Free Will

God's Choice, Our Choice

A. E. Mitchell

Onwards and Upwards Publishers

3 Radfords Turf,
Exeter EX5 7DX,
United Kingdom.
www.onwardsandupwards.org

This first edition published in the United Kingdom by Onwards and Upwards Publishers (2017).

ISBN: 978-1-78815-659-2
Typeface: Sabon LT
Graphic design: LM Graphic Design

Printed in the United Kingdom.

Endorsements

Anthony Mitchell has written a very accessible and helpful book in which he explores some essential ideas in relation to the Christian faith and life. He presents his thinking in a very straightforward way, drawing on biblical references and different ways of thinking within the Christian tradition. He explores some of these difficult tensions when seeking to understand God's will and purposes as opposed to our human will and nature. People of faith and of no faith will find this book an interesting read and it will help them in their ongoing exploration of these important matters of life and death.

The Reverend Canon Paul Seaman
Vicar
St Mary's, East Grinstead

A very useful and insightful book answering some often very challenging questions that many of us face in whatever sphere of modern life we inhabit; helpfully supported scripturally, and not avoiding difficult topics, or glossing over them or drowning them in hyperbole.

A welcome addition to any bookshelf and probably very engaging set as a lent or advent study group text.

A very reassuring book for Christians who will undoubtedly meet head on many of the questions raised in their ongoing pastoral encounters.

Revd Alex Baxter
Priest
St Barnabas Church, Bexhill-on-Sea

About the Author

Anthony was born in London but spent most of his youth in Sussex, before moving overseas where he trained to become a Maths teacher. After nearly ten years teaching he returned to the UK where he studied for and was awarded a Ph.D.

A churchgoer from a young age, Anthony attended a variety of churches whilst overseas, but only really came to realise that there was more to Christianity than attending church when he returned to England. He attended religious festivals on a regular basis, always leaving with a number of Christian books to read. He now has an extensive library of Christian literature.

Anthony has started a charity that raises funds for a community in East Africa. This work has led him to identify new ways of generating finances, including establishing himself as an author.

Contents

Free Will

Foreword by Alan Hoare

Anthony Mitchell has tackled head-on a number of issues that have puzzled and even divided Christians for centuries. And he has done it in such a way that you can tell that this is the reasoning of a man who is well matured in the Scriptures. As I read it for myself, I found three reasons why you should read it also.

Firstly, the book is very easy to read. Don't worry – it is not a deeply theological tome, but it does discuss theological issues. But he has designed it in such a way as to make theological issues easy to grasp. Anthony is good in painting a great number of scenarios that will draw the reader in, making it a lot easier to see what he is saying. Although doctrine and theology are discussed, Anthony has the knack of earthing them all to our practical experiences of life. This is a consistent pattern throughout the book.

Secondly, the way that Anthony builds his reasoning and arguments is very helpful. He leads the reader very carefully and thoroughly through a number of important issues, whilst hinting at further discussions in later chapters. He certainly knows how to whet the appetite of a serious thinker.

Thirdly, I found what Anthony has written to be very balanced and reasonable. There are areas in the book that will always be open to debate – the time frame of creation, the historicity of Job – but, as Anthony writes, these are not essentials to knowing and understanding the ways and heart of God. The prime goal of theology must always be to heighten our worship and deepen our walk with the Lord. Anthony keeps bringing all the issues back to the walking under the hand and guidance of God.

It is my feeling that this book would be most helpful to a Christian readership who are struggling in certain theological areas. I also think that it will be very helpful to an inquisitive non-Christian readership who are seeking honest answers.

Alan Hoare
Former Elim Pentecostal Pastor, Lincoln
Author and Bible Teacher

Introduction

People write books for a variety of reasons. Usually they have a real desire to write on a specific topic that they find interesting. I am not a theologian, a scientist or indeed a writer, so why have I written a book about free will?

I have become increasingly perturbed by people who pose the question: If God is good why does he allow suffering? Of course, as I am not God and am no more privy to his thoughts than anyone else, I can only speculate as to the reason or reasons. I do, however, believe that God has inspired me to put pen to paper.

I think that people who ask the question above fall into two categories: those who do not want to believe and use the question as an excuse not to pursue the Christian doctrine and those who do want to believe but find the question to be a genuine stumbling block. I hope this book touches the hearts of all those who read it and that all will find plausible explanations in what I have written.

The Bible is the source of what the Christian believes. Many people, both trained and untrained in the field of theology, have put their ideas into print. I have read the Bible from cover to cover and I study biblical passages daily. I have also read a significant quantity of Christian literature.

Before beginning the book, I wish to explain my choice of examples to illustrate many of the ideas. Where possible I use situations that relate to driving a car. I believe that, as most people reading this book drive cars, it is easy to relate to such scenarios. It is also a way of avoiding issues that could be seen as more controversial. I do also use scenarios involving money, especially VAT. I realise that these may be more controversial than those related to driving but, again, this is an area that affects many of my readers. My aim is to avoid controversy, where possible, so that you, the reader, are not distracted from the ideas that I am expounding.

I am no expert, and do not pretend to be, but I pray that you will find something in the following pages that helps you on your journey to becoming a more confident Christian.

God bless.

CHAPTER ONE

Free Will

There are many definitions of "free will". Wikipedia states:

> *Free will is the ability of agents to make choices uncon-strained by certain factors.*[1]

Indeed the article then goes on to discuss whether free will actually exists. For the purpose of this book, we will assume that it does exist in some form or other. It appears that free will allows us to do what we like, when we like and how we like. God has chosen to give us free will. In Chapter 4, I will consider possible reasons as to why this might be.

In this chapter, I consider what free will means to the individual, the motives behind many of our actions and, finally, how society tries to limit the consequences of certain actions.

What does free will mean to the individual?

Free will means that we have freedom of choice. Although certain factors may influence our decisions regarding these choices, theoretically we can do exactly what we wish at any moment in time.

As Christians, we believe that the most important decision made by anyone is whether to become a Christian. All other decisions, whether life-changing or not, are of far less significance.

Many of the major decisions common to most people depend on external factors. We need to live somewhere – a choice that may be limited by financial constraints. We have to decide whether to have a family. In this instance, we need a willing partner – not usually an

---

[1] https://en.wikipedia.org/wiki/Free_will_(disambiguation)

insurmountable obstacle! Decisions regarding employment and careers depend on education and opportunity, over which we may have some, but certainly not total, control. These major choices require considerable thought and usually do not happen instantaneously.

On a day-to-day basis, we use free will to make decisions at a personal level, many of which have little effect on anyone else. What should I wear? What shall I watch on television? What should I eat for supper? Some of these decisions do affect others. Shall I visit Mrs X in hospital or shall I go to the football? Shall I shop at the local store or use the supermarket? Shall I wait patiently in a queue of traffic or should I try to jump the queue by pushing in nearer the front?

Behind each action is a conscious or subconscious thought. Every individual on this planet has the freedom to think about whatever they wish. These thoughts are privy only to the individual and to God, unless we wish to divulge them to someone else. It is, though, our thoughts that determine our actions. Positive thoughts generally precede positive actions, whereas negative thoughts often precede negative actions.

What are the motives behind our actions?

What influences the decisions we make? I do not profess to be a psychologist but I do believe that there is one factor which influences many of the decisions we make. It is the presence of selfishness in most of our actions. Books have been written explaining that the predominant drive behind life is that of self-preservation – the preservation of our genes to ensure that they are present in succeeding generations. Animals will go to great lengths to ensure that it is their offspring that survive. Likewise, humans will also do what they can to ensure the survival of their offspring. Whether this results from the unique form of love that parents have for their children or whether there is this natural, possibly unconscious, desire to preserve our genes is not relevant here. The fact is that parents will die to save their children. Even if not called upon to go that far, parents will go to great lengths to promote the wellbeing of their offspring. Decisions regarding employment, place of residence, schools and distribution of resources often centre on the needs of the children. On occasions, when suffering financially, parents will go without food in order to ensure that their children are not hungry.

Whether or not focusing primarily on the needs of your children is regarded as selfish, humans display selfishness in many other ways. The motivation behind many acts that appear to be unselfish is often very selfish. The act of giving voluntarily appears to be very unselfish. Giving, though, is unselfish only if it is done in the way suggested in the Bible, so that only God and the donor know of the gift (Matthew 6:3). Often people give because they want to be seen to be giving. It increases their standing amongst others in society. Whilst overseas, I was watching a television station that was raising money for good causes. The names of donors appeared across the bottom of the television screen as they pledged. Often these pledges were made with the proviso that the name of the donor appeared on the screen.

A useful ploy to gain substantial amounts for a sponsored event has been to ensure that the person whose name appears first on the form is very generous. Those following will often feel obliged to match the amount. At certain times of year, especially Christmas, there may be a perceived feeling of guilt associated with enjoying a magnificent celebration and so some may give to those less fortunate as a way of appeasing that guilt. Of course, there are exceptions, and people do donate selflessly, but there may still be psychological "feel-good" factors which are hard to avoid. One of the experts questioned in *The Case for Faith* by Lee Strobel states his belief that even our good deeds are tainted by self-interest and our calls for justice are partly a desire for revenge.[2]

There are instances where humans forego their selfish desires and will act in ways which ensure that unrelated people live or have better lives because of an act of self-sacrifice. This is most obvious in the armed forces, where serving members throughout history have given their lives for their "country". Often humans put themselves at risk for the good of others without thinking of the consequences. It is those who know that they may well not survive the action they are about to take, that demonstrate the use of free will at the ultimate level. Taking this one step further, there are also "martyrs" who have given their lives for their beliefs. This is the ultimate sacrifice. It is one thing to give your life to save a fellow human or humans, but to do so for your beliefs shows commitment of the highest nature.

---

[2] Peter Kreeft in *The Case for Faith* by Lee Strobel, p.44

Each level of sacrifice, whether for a family member, a friend, someone in trouble, our country, another country, or the ultimate cause – our faith – requires an ever-greater degree of commitment. Of course, at the pinnacle of these levels is the sacrifice made by Jesus, as he knew in advance exactly what he would have to endure to achieve his goal.

Our actions are also influenced by our experiences. It is very hard to have positive thoughts if we have only had negative experiences. It is these experiences that become the foundation for our code of conduct. Most people have certain principles upon which they base their decisions and actions. These principles often have their roots in our upbringing. Without becoming embroiled in sociological arguments, it would appear that there is the need for a stable and positive environment for the years of childhood and adolescence. As youngsters, we need to learn the code of conduct that is acceptable in society in order for us to function as a productive member of that society. Many of these behaviours are uniform across all aspects of society.

How does society try to limit the consequences of certain actions?

Unfortunately, we live in a society where there are vast socioeconomic differences. There is a tendency for members of different socioeconomic groups to encourage practices, particularly in relation to their financial affairs, that should not be acceptable to society. At one end of the scale there are individuals who believe that society has a duty to support them and their families without seeing the need to earn any money. At the other end of the spectrum are those exceedingly wealthy individuals who do their utmost to avoid paying taxes.

Differences in society also result from cultural or religious beliefs. In some countries, women appear to be treated as second-class citizens. They may be forced to wear certain items of clothing. Leaders, who are male, determine what they may or may not do, whether secular or spiritual. At times, it appears that women subject to these restrictions do not wish for change, whereas others most certainly do. It is very difficult for those who believe that there should be no differential treatment between the sexes to impose their beliefs on those with very different attitudes based on culture or religion. There are signs that practices such as forcing young girls into arranged marriages are being outlawed in certain countries, but this tends to be in the more affluent countries, so may only affect those migrating to these countries. It is more difficult to persuade countries with strong cultural customs that perhaps it is time their practices changed. I have worked with a community in one such country where there is a definite desire amongst the younger women to reverse this trait. They believe that education for the young girls is the only way that they may be able to break free from this form of bondage.

Religious differences also create considerable problems and conflicts. Society requires religious tolerance. In the United Kingdom we enjoy freedom of speech, although this freedom has to ensure consideration for the beliefs and feelings of others. There are certain restrictions on what we may say. For example, quite rightly, we are not permitted to denigrate anyone on racial grounds. What is more controversial is the fact that there are moves to rewrite literature which contains characters that could be perceived to be racially orientated, one of the most famous of which occurs in certain books by Enid Blyton.

Although we cannot be prejudiced on religious grounds, there is an alarming trend to ridicule certain aspects of religion. Derisory remarks are permitted regarding our Christian God or, for example, the Muslims' Mohammed. I can accept the freedom to criticise or disagree with a faith – everyone is entitled to their opinion. Nevertheless, I cannot accept that it is right to ridicule any aspect of someone's beliefs. To me this is callous and unnecessary. I think I am correct in believing that the current Pope shares my feelings!

There are many countries in the world where individual freedom of expression is very much limited. Religious freedom, for example, does not exist in many countries. However, this immediately creates a dilemma for the Christian. Christians believe that there is only one way to eternal life and are commanded to inform all peoples of this one way. Christians are not told to bypass members of other faiths. Tolerance of other beliefs appears to be highly commendable. If, however, Christians believe that there is only one way to be saved, should they not be allowed to express this idea without fear of reprisal? It is a worry that Prince Charles has suggested that when he becomes head of the Church of England, he may become "Defender of Faiths" rather than "Defender of the Faith".

There is an ongoing debate as to which practices are permissible on the grounds of religion. Sikhs are exempt from the wearing of helmets on motorbikes. Controversially, in some workplaces Christians have been prevented from wearing crosses at work. It is often difficult to distinguish between practices that are a fundamental part of the religious beliefs and those that have become associated with a belief but are not actually a necessary component of that belief. There are practices that have been advocated on the grounds of religious beliefs in the past that would simply not be tolerated today. For instance, there appears to be evidence of child sacrifices to certain gods, including the god Baal. It is interesting to note that many of the practices regarding animal sacrifices in the Old Testament would not be permitted in most countries today. Suffice it to say, religious tolerance is a very difficult concept both for society as a whole and the individual Christian.

Another major influence on the decisions that we make is the media. Decisions are often influenced by information received from elsewhere. I shouldn't wear clothes made from animal skins. I should use an environmentally friendly mode of transport. I should eat food that has been produced without exploiting those who produce it.

At times, the number of different factors that have to be considered before making a decision can be overwhelming. I mentioned briefly how selfishness may be one motive behind charitable giving, but when we do decide to donate, we can face pressure from a multitude of sources. Many Christians recognise the biblical principle of giving a percentage of their income to the church, but depending upon the church we attend, this can vary from as little as 1 per cent to as much as 10 per cent. Charities bombard us with junk mail. Each charity supports a very worthy cause but it is difficult to give meaningfully to more than one or two. There may also be additional pressure from family and friends as to which charities we should support, and to what extent. Decisions regarding charitable giving have long-term effects on both donors and receivers.

How does society try to ensure that the actions of certain individuals do not adversely affect the lives of others?

There has to be a set of rules in place to ensure that the rights and feelings of others are respected and accommodated. Society has to live by rules and regulations. Some may argue that these may at times impede our wish to exercise free will, but most rules have been made to ensure the safety or wellbeing of the majority, for example driving on one side of the road. Driving would be impossible without such a regulation. Some laws have resulted from more arbitrary decisions, for example the age at which you are permitted to vote. Others have been introduced to supersede previous ones to accommodate a different, sometimes more modern or more sophisticated view of life. Often these rules or laws are of a more controversial nature, for example the abolition of the death penalty in the United Kingdom. Many British people would disagree with this law and other countries have retained the death penalty.

Certain regulations or laws have come about after years of confrontation and civil unrest. Consider, for example, the problems associated with the right of women to vote in Britain at the beginning of the twentieth century. More recently, we think of the anti-apartheid movement in South Africa. Overturning laws emanating from social or racial injustice where one particular group is all-powerful is extremely hard and usually comes about as a result of years of suffering by other groups not represented by the body that makes the decisions.

Other rules and regulations are introduced by successive governments, usually to ensure that they can remain in power. This may sound cynical, but whether the political party is attempting to improve the economic situation, make changes to health care or to education there is always a desire to please the majority of voters. Sometimes political parties do make unpopular decisions but the long-term aim is usually the same. Consequently, rates of and thresholds for taxation seem to change frequently – often, it appears, as and when governments perceive a degree of electoral advantage will be gained from such decisions! Of course, the legal way that we can bring about change to any law with which we disagree, at a national level, is to use our right to vote at the ballot box.

Despite what may appear to be a myriad of different rules and regulations supposedly in place for the majority of society, we do have the opportunity to exercise our free will almost continuously. There are times in life when we may decide, consciously or subconsciously, not to adhere to the law, as illustrated in the following scenario.

Driving through a sleepy village at two o'clock in the morning when the road is deserted and there is no one to be seen, it may seem perfectly acceptable to drive at 40 mph in the 30 mph zone. There are no cars on the road. There are no lights on in the houses. We may wonder why we need to drive at 30 mph under these circumstances. As the driver of the car, we may decide to ignore the speed limit. Despite the fact that we are breaking the law, we may believe our actions to be justified. Assuming there are no speed cameras, we may surmise that it is highly unlikely that anyone will notice our misdemeanour, let alone a police officer lurking in a lay-by! The fact remains that a law is being broken. The danger lies in the idea that although, in these circumstances, the perpetrator may acknowledge that a law is being broken, they are less likely to admit to committing a crime. We have the free will in all situations to decide whether to abide by the law of the land or whether to take a risk. Once we have taken a risk and escaped any consequences, we are more likely to take further risks in circumstances that are more hazardous. We need to recognise the dangers associated with breaking the law under any circumstances.

In conclusion, it should be apparent that we are exercising our right to free will almost continuously throughout the day. As mentioned at the beginning of the chapter, each human has the free will to do exactly what they like. There are both internal and external factors, both conscious and subconscious, that affect the decisions we make. Nevertheless, ultimately the individual makes the final decision. No one can override the individual's use of free will. As will be discussed later, there is one exception. God has the power to intervene and can change the decision of any individual at any time. We should remember that we do have considerable freedom to do or say as we please, but we should use this freedom constructively rather than destructively.

CHAPTER TWO

Faith in God

Before proceeding further, it is necessary to consider the concept of "faith". We need faith to believe that God exists.

What is faith?

Wikipedia states that faith is:

Complete confidence or trust in a person or thing; or a belief not based on proof.[3]

At the most basic level, faith generally results from experience. For example, we have faith in our car. We get into the car believing that it will start and that we will arrive safely at our destination, because that is what has happened in the past. Unfortunately, this faith may be misguided, as motorists do have accidents. Without this faith that the car journey will be a successful event, no one would ever venture out in their car. There are times when our faith in the driving experience may be tested. If there is ice on the road, we may have less faith in the successful outcome of the driving experience, in which case we may carry out a small risk analysis before setting off. Likewise, faith plays an important part in many other day-to-day activities.

There are some activities where we have to rely on other people, in which case we need faith in their ability, their decisions and their state of mind. This is particularly true when it comes to major surgery in hospital. Initially we would expect to be fully informed of any potential risks associated with any operation. We then need faith to have

---

[3] https://en.wikipedia.org/wiki/Faith

confidence in the reliability of the information. If we then decide to undergo surgery, we require faith in the competence of those involved in the procedure. For the more complex operations, where the risks are higher, we may wish to consult other professionals for further opinions or assessments. At times, there may be risks that are beyond the control of those performing the operation. Faith in these professionals may not be sufficient to allay our fears. Under these circumstances, we may decide to turn to a supernatural power of some type. In desperation, many who do not believe in the existence of a god do in fact offer prayers in the hope that they are wrong and there is a god who will answer them.

People are continually seeking more and more evidence before committing themselves to a belief or an idea. People are reluctant to place faith in anything without considerable evidence. At this stage it is useful to introduce a scenario.

Imagine that you are walking through the mountains in some remote corner of the world. Walking round the next corner, you notice that there is a ravine that has to be crossed by means of a rather dubious-looking bridge. The guide says the bridge was quite safe when he last used it a month ago! Quite reasonably, you ask the guide to cross first because you are uncertain as to the soundness of the bridge. You are not prepared to cross without a demonstration of some sort that the bridge is safe. By watching the guide cross safely, your faith in the soundness of the structure increases. This does not mean that you are convinced that the bridge is completely safe. You may be heavier than the guide. You may still have doubts and ask another member of the party to cross before you. As more and more people cross safely, your faith in the structure increases until eventually you decide that you are sufficiently satisfied to make the crossing yourself. Little by little, you have been seeking sufficient evidence to convince you that the bridge is safe.

Is faith enough?

In many situations, there is the desire for more than faith. For various reasons it is proof that is required. Mathematicians and scientists seek to prove theorems or establish the validity of certain outcomes. In the field of medicine, for example, it is of the utmost importance to prove not only that new drugs actually work, but also that they produce no serious side effects. It is simply not good enough for a pharmaceutical company to declare that it has "faith" in a new drug. The new drug has to undergo strict testing procedures. In the second half of the last century, a drug called thalidomide was issued to pregnant mothers without these rigorous tests for side effects, with the result that many children were born with deformed limbs. Under these circumstances, proof that something is absolutely safe is of the highest importance.

There are times, however, when we have to believe what we hear or see through communication with others. We cannot all travel to America in order to prove that it exists! We use our senses to gather enough evidence to make a judgement on what we are told. As with the bridge, where it is the sight of people crossing successfully that leads us to believe the structure to be safe, the use of one of the senses usually provides us with the desired confidence. Seeing is not always believing! Illusionists can create situations where things appear to happen but in fact they do not.

It would appear that the higher the potential risk associated with any given situation, the greater the amount of evidence required before we become convinced. In many situations we have to accept the word of someone else, in which case the more we trust an individual the less the additional proof we require to accept what we are told. Unfortunately, there are people who provide false information in order to persuade others to have faith in what they are asking them to do. Many people have been persuaded to hand over money to support scams in which they have had faith.

What sort of faith leads to a belief in God?

So how do people come to believe in God? Faith in God is not dissimilar to believing in anything else. Most people require proof of some sort that God exists before making any commitment. Unfortunately, it is not usually possible to have a sensual experience concerning God. Very few of us are fortunate enough to see or hear God on a personal level.

I do believe that God has spoken to me directly on at least one occasion, the most notable of which changed my life. I had been living and working overseas for a considerable length of time and for various reasons I had reached the stage where I had no idea what to do next. I was actually working on someone's boat when, all of a sudden, I felt a definite call from God to return to England. It was a strange experience, but at the time I had no doubt that this was what God wanted. It was contrary to what I had expected and I had no idea as to the nature of his plans. As I was convinced that God had spoken to me, I decided to put my trust in his intervention. Although my life has had its ups and downs, looking back on that moment, there is no doubt in my mind that it was the right decision.

People may provide details of encounters with God, where they believe God has appeared to them in some form through a dream or vision. The listener, however, has to rely on the integrity of not only the person reporting the encounter but also the particular interpretation of what actually happened. More often than not, commitment to the Christian set of beliefs comes after a lengthy assessment of arguments for and against those beliefs.

Beyond our comprehension

Before considering some facts that support the existence of God, it is worth pointing out that it is the very nature of God that provides the greatest obstacle to belief in his existence. Faith in God involves believing in the existence of a phenomenon that is beyond the comprehension of rationality. There is nothing in our world that can be compared with God. Those who believe in God have to believe that there is an extra dimension to life. Life is more than what can be experienced through the senses – sight, sound, touch, smell and taste. For many people this requires a considerable leap of faith. As R.T. Kendall states in his book *Pure Joy*, "Faith is trusting in God without empirical evidence … Faith is believing without seeing."[4] The Bible tells us, "Faith is being certain of what we do not see" (Hebrews 11:1). Peter Kreeft suggests that God provides just enough evidence so that those who want to follow the clues can find him.[5]

The journey to an assurance of the existence of God and a profound belief in the Christian doctrine is often very rocky, with many highs and lows. I would like to propose five arguments that support the notion that our Christian God does exist. The first two – creation and the nature of the human mind – appear to point to the existence of a

---

[4] *Pure Joy*, R.T. Kendall, p.31
[5] Kreeft in Strobel, p.33

supernatural being of some type. The remaining three – the Bible, Jesus and the disciples – appear to confirm that this being is in fact the God that Christians worship.

Creation

Creation is a topic that has attracted a significant amount of attention, particularly since the latter half of the nineteenth century. How exactly did life begin and how did the animals and plants that we know today come to exist? For some time there have been two extremes to the debate. Either God created the world as set out in Genesis or else animals and plants evolved over millions of years. In support of the latter argument, biologists can explain how different species could have evolved from single-celled organisms.

There are problems with both points of view. The creation story in Genesis is very simplistic and, if taken literally, things happened very quickly. However, animals and plants appear to have evolved in an ordered fashion, which suggests some sort of guiding influence. It is this sense of order that has led me to believe that in fact rather than there being two extremes to the argument, the two ideas support each other. It is well worth reading *Creation or Evolution* by Denis Alexander, who argues that the two perceived extremes of evolution and creation should be regarded as complementing rather than contradicting each other. He suggests that the world was not created in seven twenty-four hour days but was created by God over a period of time.

There appears to be sufficient scientific evidence to suggest that the sequence of events as depicted in Genesis should be taken seriously, provided that we do not associate the word "day" with a period of twenty-four hours. I discuss the various interpretations surrounding words used in the Bible in Chapter 8.

The sense of order in the evolutionary process does appear to require some sort of guidance from a superior being. I am not a scientist or a theologian but it is worth mentioning a few points that lend credence to this idea.

Statisticians will tell you that the chances of a planet having the conditions to support life as we know it are infinitesimally small. This is perhaps the main reason why, as yet, no other planet that supports life has been identified. In *The Case for Faith* by Lee Strobel and also in *The Case for God* by Peter S. Williams, there is considerable discussion surrounding not only the probability that a planet can support life but also that life could form of its own accord. In *The Case for God*, Peter Williams also discusses the complexities surrounding DNA. He cites arguments that suggest its nature is such that the possibilities of its evolution and construction purely by chance appear to be miniscule. The conclusion in both cases is that there is the need for an "intelligent designer". The notion of the involvement of an "intelligent designer" has been an issue for discussion and debate since the time of Thomas Aquinas in the thirteenth century. Despite new revelations in the scientific field, there is still the feeling that studying science will bring you closer to God.

Once the correct conditions have been established and life has begun, it appears that there needs to be some logical progression from single-celled organisms to more complex creatures. Do we really believe that this can happen by chance without any form of guidance from a creator? There are theories as to how new species developed over millions of years, but this does not contradict the idea of an ordered development overseen by a creator. To the uninformed layman, it is extremely hard to comprehend how ants and elephants may have developed from the same original single-celled organisms without any guidance.

There are further mysteries. It has been suggested that the need to evade predators may have led to the development of winged species. This raises a number of questions: How did these organisms come to realise that wings were needed? How were wings developed? Wings will only function if fully developed, in which case, how did the organisms know that the development would work eventually? Undoubtedly there are biologists who can supply answers to these questions, but these responses are at best speculation and it is most unlikely that anyone will be able to supply definitive proof as to exactly how and why winged creatures developed.

Certain species of plant rely on one specific insect to ensure that they can reproduce, and often it is a two-way relationship in that the insect also needs that particular plant. In some instances, timing can be crucial. The juvenile form of many insects has no adult present when it hatches to teach it what it must do in order to survive. There is some innate mechanism which ensures that the majority of these juveniles not only hatch at just the moment that is most beneficial to their survival, but also guides them to feast on the food that is vital for their development.

When considering the various organs within each organism that function together to ensure its survival, it is difficult to see how they could have developed without some sort of guidance. Consider the eye, for example. At some stage, a need to be able to see must have triggered this development, but the eye itself is highly complex. Denis Alexander explains how the eye could have developed into the sophisticated organ that we know today. It is a very logical process, but the fact that the process is so logical seems to indicate that some sort of guiding influence was present to oversee the development. Even if there had been a considerable amount of trial and error in a process that took years to perfect the organism as we know it today, it is hard to believe that each improvement happened by chance rather than by guidance.

The ear is another very complex organism. What actually happened to trigger the creation of the ear? Arguments regarding the need to be able to hear the approach of predators may well be valid, but something has to realise that predators make a noise. Once it has been established that noise exists, how does an organism begin to create something that will enhance this noise? The ear is an extremely sophisticated device, which if invented today would make someone exceedingly wealthy. Could it really have developed without any divine guidance? This is what those who refuse to acknowledge the presence of a creator god would wish us to believe.

The body has many parts that appear to have achieved the ultimate in efficiency. The penis, for example, serves two purposes. In its normal state, it is the means by which the male body passes urine. In its erect state, it is the mechanism by which sperm is ejected for the reproductive process. The need for two separate organs has been removed.

There are many complex organs in the body and the fact that they work in complete harmony (most of the time!) is an achievement of which any engineer would be extremely proud. It is worth pausing for a moment to contemplate the wonders of the human body.

On one of the many occasions when I was deliberating on the contents of a particular section of this book, I happened to be walking in the woods locally with my dog. I suddenly stopped walking and realised exactly what I was doing. My thoughts were miles away and yet, through my eyes my brain was subconsciously ensuring that my legs were moving in such a way that I was walking without slipping or stumbling on the path. So much of what we do daily is the result of subconscious actions that are initiated by the brain, but of which we are unaware. Can we really believe this extraordinary machine that is our body has been created purely by chance, without any intervention from an intelligent designer?

An interesting corollary to these thoughts concerns speculation as to what would have happened had one of the senses not developed. What if the sense of hearing, and consequently talking, had never developed in any species? Communication would have been limited to sign language and the written word. Watching, for example, a hammer striking a nail, would someone at some stage have believed that the concept of sound did in fact exist but no one had the facility to hear it? Would someone then have developed an artificial means of hearing? The point behind this speculation concerns the possibility that an additional sense exists that has not yet been discovered because no species has developed a means of perceiving it, or maybe one or more species have, but it has not been recognised by humans.

As already mentioned, the fact remains that many people do not believe in the existence of God and are prepared to accept that creation took place by chance. For me and for many Christians it is the sheer complexity and magnificent efficiency of organs such as the eye, the ear and the brain that leads us to believe that there must be some supernatural being responsible for overseeing the construction of the individual organs in such a way that they function in the way that they do. Perhaps one day scientists will be able to construct an eye or an ear or even a brain, but at present it is beyond even the most skilled technicians. Computers can be programmed to perform complex tasks and may appear to think for themselves, but they require a programmer in order to function. These programmers will continue to develop more highly sophisticated computers, but these computers will continue to rely exclusively on their programmers in order to develop. Does this not serve to illustrate the same need for a creator of some sort who has overseen not only the creation of individual organisms that function at the highest level of efficiency, but also the development of a vast variety of organisms that work together to ensure the sustainability of the planet? Species have disappeared and others have emerged but, surely, is this not part of some vast plan, the knowledge of which will always remain a mystery to those living on the planet?

The next time you walk in the woods, pick up an acorn, examine it carefully and then look at a tall oak tree. The oak tree came from an acorn similar to the one in your hand. It is difficult to believe that the transition from acorn to oak tree is possible solely due to a series of events that have happened over millions of years without the guidance of a creator.

I remember the day that I decided, for the first time, to plant some seeds in a small area of my garden that had been rather neglected. I had had the seeds for some time. I believe they had originally been attached to the inside of a well-known brand of cereal! Consequently, I had no idea whether they would grow. I prepared the area thoroughly and then planted the tiny seeds. I watered the patch daily. Eventually one tiny growth appeared with two very small leaves. Initially I had no idea whether it was friend or foe, plant or weed, so I continued to water the patch.

Despite planting a considerable number of seeds, nothing else appeared. I nurtured the single growth and watched it increase in size. Eventually it produced its first flower, after which there was no stopping it. It must have had at least twenty flowers at one stage. Out of the tiny seed emerged this wonderful plant with its beautiful flowers. Although not so incredible to many gardeners, who see this amazing phenomenon occurring time after time, this was indeed incredible to me. To witness this considerable growth emerging from the smallest of seeds seemed to illustrate the power of God in creation. Each little plant is a miraculous illustration of the wonders of the natural world.

Of course, we only have to observe via a microscope the uniting of a human sperm and an egg to wonder at the chain of events that this initiates to provide a new human being. All creatures start life in the same way. They develop from the most miniscule of beginnings. Are we to believe that this incredible process has been developed and perfected through an evolutionary progression as a consequence of chance alone?

The nature of the human mind

The second point I wish to make supporting the notion of the existence of a supernatural being concerns the predetermination of humans to believe that such a being (or beings) exists. John Calvin, in the sixteenth century, was one of the first to advance the idea that God had indeed endowed humans with an inbuilt sense which perceived the existence of a divine being. Throughout history, different civilisations have had their own god or gods to worship. As explorers discovered previously unknown tribes of people living in different countries, they found beliefs in the existence of some form of supernatural being (or beings). It is as if humans are preconditioned to believe in the supernatural.

The majority of, if not all, traits exhibited by humans have a function, but what is the point of supernatural belief if the supernatural does not exist? It would appear to be totally unnecessary. We are supposedly rational creatures, so why should we believe in something that is completely irrational unless it exists? Our thought processes seem to have developed far beyond those of other creatures. From the studies of even the most intelligent creatures, all actions appear to have a purpose. Why should humans be different? Why should they be prone to beliefs that are meaningless? It is often argued that a belief in a god serves as a psychological prop to those who struggle through life. True, we have vivid imaginations and can readily fantasise, but the vast majority of people can tell the difference between fantasy and fact. Clinging to a belief in something that is fantastic can readily be realised as such. Why do so many humans have this innate desire to believe in something that is supernatural? Have we been totally misled? Given the discussion in the previous section where all the parts of our body function harmoniously, it seems bizarre to have one aspect of our thinking that is illogical and irrational.

There does appear to be an increasing number of people who consider belief in any form of supernatural being to be old-fashioned and outmoded. They believe that eventually everything will have a logical rather than supernatural explanation but, as mentioned earlier, many of those who profess to have no supernatural beliefs will resort to prayer at times of extreme trauma or tragedy. Non-believers have confessed to using prayer as a last resort because all else appears to have failed. Why this sudden appeal to someone not of this world? Surely this demonstrates an innate attraction to a supernatural force which is there because it has been placed there by a supernatural being. It could be that everyone has this seed planted within. For some it may lie dormant and never grow. For others it eventually germinates and there follows a belief in some form of deity. As Christians, we believe that God planted that seed and that ultimately everyone will eventually, by some means, become aware of his existence. C.S. Lewis suggested that there is a deep and intense feeling of longing within human beings which nothing of earthly experience can satisfy.[6] Or, in the famous words of Augustine (speaking of God), "You have made us for yourself, and our hearts are restless until they rest in you."[7]

These first two arguments appear to support the idea that a supernatural being (or beings) does exist. The next three arguments support the idea that this being is in fact the God who is central to the Christian faith.

The Bible

There is a book called the Bible which is probably the most remarkable book in the world. The first part of this book, the Old Testament, was written by and for a very small community in the ancient world. True, the Israelites were powerful and prosperous for a short time, but for most of their history they were ruled by other nations of far greater power. It is interesting that these powerful nations have been consigned to the pages of history, whereas the Jewish race survives to this day. Does this alone not single them out as being of some importance? Why and how have they managed to survive, when so often they have almost been obliterated? Not only have powerful nations like the Greeks and the Romans risen and fallen over the years but also their gods have long since been denounced as meaningless. The Jewish people have never achieved the powerful status of many of the great empires and yet it is the book containing the history of this particular race that has assumed such great importance. It is the relationship with their God that has achieved this incredible status in the world today. Granted, over the past 2,000 years, the story of Jesus and the addition of the books that form the New Testament have assisted in raising its profile. Nevertheless, the whole book is still regarded as being of great importance. Does the fact that this particular book has survived not point to the existence of someone who is determined to ensure its survival? There will be more about the Bible in Chapter 8.

---

[6] *Christian Theology – An Introduction* by Alister E. McGrath, p.150
[7] McGrath, p.149

Jesus, the Son of God

The second point concerns Jesus, the Son of God. It is perhaps the story contained in the New Testament that most Christians will use to support the idea that the Christian God exists. There are two aspects to this idea. Is (or was) Jesus a real person? If he exists (or existed), is (or was) he really the Son of God?

I am of the opinion that the number of people who do not believe that Jesus exists (or existed) is perhaps less than is often suggested. It is actually the reluctance of people to accept what Jesus said about himself that prevents them from becoming Christians. There are writers whose works are not part of the Bible who record the fact that Jesus was indeed a real person. Josephus and Tacitus are two of these. It would seem that a significant number of non-Christians are happy to accept Jesus as a historical figure, perhaps even acknowledging that he was a very good man with some excellent ideas as to how people should function as members of society. It is, perhaps, the consequences of acknowledging the idea that Jesus was possibly more than just a "good man" that has caused non-Christians to avoid investigating the idea more fully. Speaking of the resurrection of Jesus, David Pawson says:

> The eye-witness testimony plus the circumstantial evidence is far stronger that the evidence that Julius Caesar invaded England in 55 BC. But the problem is that if Jesus rose from the dead, then people know they have to change their lives ... You can't ignore Jesus, but you can ignore Julius Caesar.[8]

Indeed, it is the idea that Jesus could well be much more than a "good man" that is the real stumbling block. It requires a considerable leap of faith and the consequential commitment to the Christian beliefs if we are to acknowledge that Jesus was and still is the Son of God. As C.S. Lewis suggests in *Mere Christianity* – either Jesus was and still is the Son of God, in which case all that he said and did as reported in the Bible is true and must be taken seriously, or Jesus was a nutcase and should have been forgotten quickly. There is no room for any stance somewhere in between. If Jesus was simply a "good man" with some sound ideas, then he would not have declared himself to be the Son of God. "Good men" cannot be good if they make such absurd claims,

---

[8] *Unlocking the Bible* by David Pawson, p.642

even if it is believed that Jesus was perhaps just deluded or mistaken in his beliefs. Since Jesus, how many other "good men" have made similar statements regarding their possible status as the Son of God and are still remembered and worshipped today? None! Surely this implies there must be real validity in Jesus' claim!

There is something that is unique about Jesus and supports the idea that he was, and still is, more than just a very special person. As every Christian will tell you, Jesus was crucified, rose from the dead and then appeared to his disciples. This is not only the rock on which the whole Christian faith depends but it appears to be unique in the history of humankind. There are stories in the Bible of people who were raised from the dead, for instance Lazarus and the daughter of Jairus. Unlike Jesus, these people simply resumed their lives as normal human beings. Jesus' resurrection was unique in that he returned as a physical being but in some way his physique and appearance had changed. He was not immediately recognisable to his followers, both when he suddenly appeared in a locked room and again when he joined two of his disciples on the road to Emmaus.

The death and resurrection of Jesus is so fundamental to the Christian belief that it is one of the few facts about Jesus that appears in detail in all four Gospels. It is also discussed at length in the letters that make up the remainder of the New Testament. However, it is the resurrection of Jesus that creates possibly the biggest problem for non-believers. As mentioned earlier, people are happy with things that appear to be rational. When faced with ideas that seem to be irrational or supernatural, they become uneasy. It is hard to accept the concept that someone can die and yet three days later come back to life. The answer lies in the nature of God. God is a supernatural being. We are not supernatural. It is therefore difficult for us to understand his actions and some of the reasons behind those actions. We can only examine the evidence and reach our own conclusions.

There was a purpose behind the crucifixion and subsequent resurrection of Jesus. Jesus died so that those who believe in him could receive forgiveness for their sins. Although it is not immediately obvious to many Christians why Jesus actually had to die, we are told that God had to offer a perfect sacrifice in order to be able to forgive all those who have sinned and wish to repent of their sins. Jesus had to be that sacrifice because he was the only perfect being to have walked on this planet.

Before continuing, it is worth considering the purity of Jesus more carefully. We are led to believe, quite correctly, that the Bible is a special book, in many cases recounting stories of very special people. We might therefore expect to read about the lives of several people whose lives appeared to be faultless. In fact, this is not the case. The great heroes of the Old Testament, such as Abraham, Moses and David, had flaws in their characters. At some stage in their lives, each and every one did at least one thing that displeased God and revealed a deficiency. The knowledge that these great men were not perfect serves two important functions. It shows that God does not require his people to be perfect in order that he can use them, which is good news for us! It also highlights how difficult it is to be perfect and therefore reinforces the uniqueness of Jesus.

Returning to the death and resurrection of Jesus, it is the fact that Jesus rose from the dead that differentiates Christianity from all other religions. In other religions, gods or prophets who have led exemplary lives are followed. Believers are then required to imitate these "good" lives as closely as possible to attain a series of rewards. In contrast, Christians are asked simply to believe that Jesus did what he did and is who he is in order to obtain forgiveness. Accepting Jesus into our lives obviously has consequences for how we then behave, but it is belief rather than deeds that is the key.

Transformed lives

My third and final point regarding the existence of the Christian God relates to what happened once Jesus had risen from the dead and ascended to heaven. His followers, known as his disciples, were completely shattered by the crucifixion. They had believed that Jesus was the leader who was going to make things happen. Reading about the healings, the miracles and the teachings of Jesus, we can see why the disciples were convinced that Jesus was the Son of God. He then allowed himself to be crucified without any resistance. Despite having been warned by Jesus himself that his crucifixion and subsequent resurrection would take place, the disciples had not been able to comprehend what was happening. They were totally devastated and disillusioned when Jesus died. It did not occur to them that the man who had performed the miracles could possibly rise from the dead, even though he was the Son of God and he had said that he would. When

Jesus was arrested, the disciples disappeared. Peter tried to stay close, but even his courage deserted him. The disciples believed that Jesus was dead and that they had been mistaken in their assessment of his status. They could not accept that Jesus was the Messiah and had allowed himself to die in such a terrible manner. The disciples were so afraid that they too would be arrested, that they hid behind locked doors. It is safe to say that they were at rock bottom.

Then something dramatic took place, something so phenomenal that the lives of the disciples changed for ever. This event would have to have been something truly unique. It was! Jesus rose from the dead! The experience was mind-blowing, so much so that these followers who had initially been so timid and full of despair became different people. They were now so convinced that Jesus was the Son of God that they spent the rest of their lives ensuring that the news about Jesus was spread as far and wide as possible. The change in those disciples was incredible. One minute they had been timid and frightened for their own safety, the next they were so full of confidence that they were prepared to suffer and die for what they knew to be the truth. Only an event such as the resurrection could have had such an impact on their lives. Not only did the death and resurrection of Jesus achieve God's purpose but it also ensured that there was a group of people on earth who would spend the remainder of their lives spreading the news about Jesus, no matter what the consequences to themselves. The example set by the disciples has been replicated by many others since.

Speaking of the origins of the Christian movement in his book *Who Moved the Stone?* Frank Morison asks:

> *Does this rather heterogeneous body of simple folk, reeling under the shock of the crucifixion, the utter degrading and death of their leader, look like the driving force we require? ... Something came into the lives of these very simple and ordinary men which transformed them.*[9]

In fact, the reactions of the disciples and their conviction that Jesus is the Son of God have led many people since to devote their lives to the Christian beliefs. There are many cases of people being tortured and/or dying for these beliefs. I stated earlier that dying for our beliefs requires a level of devotion beyond the reach of many people. There has to be a

---

[9] *Who Moved the Stone?* by Frank Morison, p.115-116

deep conviction that what we believe is the truth. Today Christians continue to be persecuted and killed for their beliefs. Surely, neither a disciple alive at the time of Jesus nor a devoted Christian at a later time would die for something that they did not believe was the absolute truth.

In conclusion, I believe that there is sufficient evidence in these five arguments to convince those reading this book to explore and contemplate the issues further. We have the free will to assess the arguments as we wish and then draw our own conclusions. For those who accept that God does exist, the next chapter endeavours to explain some of his characteristics.

CHAPTER THREE

God

It is important to consider a few points regarding the nature of God before proceeding further, as he is unique and is the foundation upon which the Christian faith is built.

I believe that anyone who writes anything about God or who tries to explain who he is or what he does needs to be very humble and acknowledge that as humans we can only offer limited ideas and speculations. God is so superior to humans that endeavouring to unravel the mysteries of God has been likened to trying to teach an ant how to use a computer.

We must acknowledge that all humans have limitations, whereas God does not. It may often be difficult to define these limitations. For example, athletes continue to break records. At one time, it was thought that being able to run a hundred metres in less than ten seconds was impossible, but this happens quite regularly now. Will an athlete ever be able to break the nine-second or eight-second or even seven-second barrier? We might suppose that seven seconds is impossible, but who knows? In the sphere of knowledge, scientists continually strive to make new discoveries and it would be very foolish to predict any limitations as to what may be established. However, our knowledge concerning God will always be very limited. We must accept this as being a fact.

It is also a mistake to attempt to describe God in human terms. He does not operate under the same restrictions and limitations as humans. He can defy the laws of science. For God nothing is impossible. He can perform miracles as and when he wishes. As humans, we have no right to question his agenda. When God intervenes in a particular way, his reasoning may not be immediately apparent, but we have to believe that it is part of his plan for our lives. There will come a time when all will be revealed. We can say that God is perfect. As mentioned in the previous chapter, no human is perfect and the only perfect person to live on this planet was Jesus, who was unique.

Through the Bible God reveals certain of his characteristics. I would like to focus on three "omnis", as I believe these to be particularly relevant to the subject of this book. God is omnipotent, omnipresent and omniscient.

God is omnipotent

Omnipotent means that God is all-powerful. He has greater power than any other being, whether natural or supernatural. This infers that he has authority over everyone, including Satan. I discuss Satan and the concept of evil in the next chapter. If God wants to do something or he wishes an event to take place, it will. No one can intervene to prevent it. There have been times in the past when powerful leaders and dictators have appeared to wield unprecedented power, some of whom have continued to have a major influence even after they have died. Such power is still insignificant compared to the power of God.

The most obvious illustration of this power concerns the resurrection of Jesus from the dead. No human will ever achieve anything of such magnitude. Certain people have had their bodies frozen, believing that one day scientists will find a way of bringing people back to life. Scientists may well be able to prolong life, with people being able to live for 150 years or more in years to come. However, no species will ever become immortal in this world as we know it at present, as that contravenes the laws of nature and of God. Immortality is for the next life.

On a more personal level, God can change the course of the life of any human, should that human ask him to. At times, he will also intervene to change lives without being asked, as he did with Saul on the road to Damascus, but this is not the norm unless God has a special plan for the individual that necessitates such an intervention. Generally, it is the individual who asks God.

God continues to intervene in the lives of many people on a daily basis, often by speaking to them directly. I mentioned in the previous chapter that I believe God has intervened in my life. There is no doubt that such an intervention has a profound effect on a believer. Many

Christians have had revelations or experienced events that have convinced them of the existence of God. Miraculous healing does still occur. When reading inspirational biographies of Christians through the ages, we can clearly see God's intervention in their lives. Things happened that, if occurring once might be considered a coincidence or lucky, but because they happened again and again, I feel that there must have been some sort of divine intervention.

The whys and wherefores concerning God's intervention in the lives of his people is an important subject, about which I hope to offer some useful ideas during the course of this book. As shall be discussed later in greater depth, it is the fact that God has chosen to give all humans free will that limits his intervention. It is never correct to say that God cannot intervene in a specific situation. Instead, most of the time he has chosen not to intervene. However, God is still omnipotent and in absolute control.

God is omnipresent

God is also omnipresent. This means literally that God is everywhere, in all places at the same time. To believe this, we must reject the idea that God is some sort of advanced human. Humans, however advanced, cannot be in more than one place at a time. The Bible states in Genesis 1:26, that God made humans in his own image, but that does not mean either that God is in any way human or that we, as humans, possess the attributes of God. Having the ability to be everywhere at the same time allows God to be with every one of his followers all the time. He can react to any request instantly. This may be very difficult to comprehend, but Christians have to accept that omnipresence is an attribute of God without trying to understand how it is achieved. Some have tried to suggest that all believers have little guardian angels to watch over them. These angels supposedly know God's will and can react accordingly. This explanation may appear to help some people with the concept of omnipresence. Unfortunately, it tries to explain omnipresence in human terms and does not accept the fact that God is a superior being who has the ability to be in all places at the same time.

Free Will

God is omniscient

The third attribute is that of omniscience. Omniscience means all-knowing. God knows everything. In fact, God knows everything even before it happens. God knew everything that has happened before it happened, knows everything that is happening before it happens and knows everything that will happen before it happens. The implications are considerable. God knowing exactly what will occur in the future implies that nothing can be done to change the future. Nothing that happens on earth can change the sequence of events that God knows will eventuate.

This immediately raises a multitude of questions. God asks us to pray. Many prayers are petitions for change. If nothing will change the course of events, then what is the point of prayer? The response is actually quite straightforward. God knows in advance exactly when each individual is going to pray and what the individual will request. He also knows how the prayer will be answered before the prayer is uttered. God does not wonder whether a Christian will pray. He knows the answer in advance! He asks Christians to pray because he wishes to answer their prayers, although not always in the way that they might wish. In Chapter 6, I consider in detail how God answers prayers. The fact that God knows what is about to happen does not preclude Christians from praying.

Another issue raised by God's omniscience concerns disasters at both a personal and national level. People may ask why God allows disasters of any kind to take place if he knows they are going to happen. This is discussed in detail in Chapter 5. At present, it is sufficient to accept that God is omniscient and knows exactly what will happen in the future. Notice that I have used the word "knows" what will happen, which is not the same as "ordains" what will happen. I do not believe that God causes a natural disaster that kills thousands of people, or even just a few people. I also believe that God does not specifically instigate the death of any individual. As this is an issue of relevance throughout the book, I would like to pause in order to clarify this point.

There are passages in the Old Testament such as Exodus 13:15, 1 Samuel 15:2-3 and 2 Samuel 6:7, and one particular passage in the New Testament, Acts 5:5-10, that seem to contradict this idea. I do not profess to be a biblical scholar and so can only offer possible explanations regarding these passages.

Much of the Old Testament, as was mentioned earlier, tells the story of the Jewish people and how they survived, often under very difficult circumstances, with the help of God. Because life was tough, God expected his people to follow a code of conduct that, if disobeyed, resulted in harsh penalties, some of which included death. Also, when other nations stood in the way of God's plans, they had to be dealt with severely. For example, the Egyptians would not allow the Israelites to leave peacefully and so God was particularly severe on them. So yes, in the Old Testament, God permitted people to die so that his people could survive. In Chapter 10 I will discuss in greater detail God's use of war and conflict in the Old Testament.

On the other hand, by the time of the New Testament, God has revealed himself through Jesus to be a God of love. A loving God cannot possibly kill people in order to achieve his desires. I believe that the last person God decreed should die for a specific purpose was Jesus Christ. After that, things changed.

What about the passage in Acts mentioned previously? It is interesting that both verses say that Ananias and Sapphira "fell down and died". It does not say that God caused them to die. I believe that both Ananias and Sapphira may have suffered heart attacks brought on by shock. Once each had realised the enormity of the sin of their deception, they collapsed and died. Yes, their deaths were a warning as to what could happen to anyone who tried to deceive God, but I believe that God did not kill either of them. It is important to reiterate that God is a God of love. Although he may not intervene to prevent people dying, I believe that God never ordains the death of anyone. This has important ramifications that will be discussed in the remaining chapters.

Returning to the issues of this chapter, although God has many other attributes, the three that I have highlighted appear to demonstrate that God is more powerful than any other being, can be everywhere at once and knows exactly what will happen. He is in outright control of everything. Nothing escapes his attention. He can intervene at any time, so why does he not intervene more often, especially when some horrific event is about to occur? Before looking at this, I propose to consider the whole concept of evil and possible reasons why evil is permitted in God's world.

Free Will

CHAPTER FOUR

God and Evil

God has provided us with all we need to live a "perfect" life on this planet. We have the ideal environmental conditions in which to live. The fact that this may not appear to be the case in all countries may well be due more to decisions made by humans than to the environment itself. We have animals and plants that interact in such a way that we can live. We have a code of conduct, the Bible, which explains exactly how humans should interact. If every individual chose to become a Christian and followed this code of conduct, many of the problems in society would disappear. God has given us the "blueprint" for life.

It has often been stated by both Christians and non-Christians that they cannot understand why, if God is good, he permits evil. What is actually implied is the question: Why does God allow anything bad or unpleasant to happen to his people whom he says he loves?

What is "evil"?

In this chapter, I will try to put forward some ideas as to why there has to be evil in the world. Before doing so, it is important to consider what is meant by "evil".

Humans tend to regard people who have overseen horrendous events as being evil, for example Adolf Hitler. We think that acts such as murder and rape are evil. Evil is anything that is at the far end of a spectrum of deeds that goes from good to bad. As Christians, we have been introduced to a different word – sin. In God's eyes, anything that contravenes his code of conduct is regarded as a sin, whether this is a major misdemeanour such as murder or a comparatively minor one such as looking at another human lustfully.

We may find the fact that God does not differentiate between "major" and "minor" misdemeanours extremely difficult to comprehend. It is certainly much easier for us to forgive someone who reverses into our car leaving a small dent in the bumper than someone who races through a red light and causes our car to be written off! To God, there is little difference – sin is sin.

As explained in the introduction, I am using situations relating to driving a car and money as my primary source of illustrations. This is particularly relevant regarding sin. I am using speeding and VAT avoidance as my two main examples. Many reading this book may believe they have never committed a "serious sin" and also believe that they do not break the law. I would reiterate that, as suggested in the first chapter, although it may not be regarded as a serious crime, everyone who drives has probably at some time exceeded the speed limit and therefore committed a crime. By using speeding, I can make these discussions relevant to most. Similarly, many readers will have at some stage payed "cash in hand" to a tradesman, thus avoiding paying VAT. Again, this may not be perceived as anything too dire, but it is breaking the law and it is sinning.

In order to avoid concern about perceived degrees of seriousness of any particular "sin" or anything "bad", I will use the word "unpleasant" as a generic term to denote anything that can be perceived as bad, negative or disagreeable in the eyes of any particular human, as well as what is sinful in the eyes of God. I believe that whereas the word "evil" is too strong for some of the examples that follow, the word "unpleasant" caters for all manner of situations.

I intend to propose four arguments that support the existence of unpleasantness in the world, the first two of which are closely related and look at the world as we know it. The second two are also closely related, but directly involve our relationship with God. I will then consider the necessity for the presence of evil if God wishes us to have free will.

Before proceeding further, I must clarify one more important issue. Those reading this book are likely to have very diverse beliefs regarding the creation story and the ideas surrounding the concept of "original sin". This book is not the place to argue for or against any specific viewpoint. Whether or not there was a moment in time when only two people existed, living in a world without sin is not relevant to the discussion. I will, though, refer to the possibility that such a state of affairs may have existed when considering the various arguments.

An absence of unpleasantness

My first argument is in the form of a question. Is it possible for human beings to exist and function in an environment where there is no unpleasantness?

Our initial response might well be, "Of course it is!" Humans could be pleasant to each other; we could be unselfish and think of others. Surely it is possible for people to live in harmony with each other? Surely our world could function without diseases and disasters? Unfortunately, as I hope to illustrate, this is not quite as straightforward as it may first appear.

We need to consider the realities more carefully. The biggest obstacle is death. What about death? Maybe there was a time in the Garden of Eden when the concept of eternal life here on earth was a reality. There was to be no death. Unfortunately, the planet as we know it cannot function without death. Creatures and plants have to die. Humans have to die. This planet is overpopulated at present, so how can we envisage the scenario where everyone who ever lived would still be alive? In the crudest terms, people have to die to make room for others! It is suggested in the Bible that Noah lived for 950 years (Genesis 9:29). Such a lifespan is incredible. If we humans continued to live so long, how could the planet support us? As it is, at present the world appears to be overpopulated. It is difficult to contemplate a state of affairs where all those born after the year 1200 would still be alive. In all probability, Henry III would still be the King of England and all those who followed would still be waiting for him to die!

How can there be death without unpleasantness? Even if everyone was assigned a finite lifespan, after which they died peacefully, there would still be the unpleasantness for family and friends associated with the death of a loved one. Where there is death, there must be a degree of unpleasantness.

This is perhaps more easily recognised when considering pets. At present, the most common pets – cats and dogs – usually live for between twelve and twenty years. Although those of us who have pets acknowledge the fact that they will die after this comparatively short lifespan, we enjoy their company while they live and are willing to suffer the heartbreak of their death. The death of a beloved pet is extremely unpleasant. It is difficult to imagine the conditions under which the situation could change. Those of us who enjoy the companionship of cats, dogs or any other pet would have to do without them if the trauma associated with their loss was to be avoided.

Death is perhaps an insurmountable obstacle when it comes to contemplating a world without unpleasantness, but I wish to consider other factors that seem to preclude any form of utopia here on earth.

Do we have to experience natural disasters such as earthquakes and tsunamis? Is there a need for extreme weather conditions that involve drought, floods or hurricanes? I do not purport to understand the constitution of our planet, but there is a chance that many natural disasters are necessary to achieve some sort of equilibrium in the forces that sustain its status quo. Bush fires in Australia, for example, are necessary to promote new growth. Some disasters may have been caused inadvertently by the actions of humans but, as yet, we do not understand enough about their origins to rectify the situation. This is explored in more detail in Chapter 5. Many natural disasters are caused by extreme weather conditions. What is the ideal weather? Perhaps it should be warm during the day and rain at night, but much of nature requires more extreme weather conditions. Certain animals and plants need extreme weather in order to flourish. In the Garden of Eden, the weather was such that Adam and Eve were naked, but could these weather conditions really be sustained if life on the planet was to function efficiently? I consider the weather again later when looking at God's answers to prayer in Chapter 6.

We live in an environment with other creatures and plants, many of which depend on each other for their nourishment. It is often regarded as unpleasant watching an animal hunting down its prey and then tearing it apart in order to eat it. Again, there is a suggestion in Genesis that humans and all animals may once have been vegetarians. This would eliminate the need for this source of unpleasantness, but may lead to other problems regarding the profligacy of certain creatures. No matter how harsh the hunting and killing of prey may seem, it does assist in ensuring a certain balance between species which could only otherwise be sustained by natural disasters, like droughts to kill off the vast numbers of animals that would have overpopulated certain areas. As C.S. Lewis says in *The Problem of Pain:*

Try to exclude the possibility of suffering which the order of nature and the existence of free-wills involve, and you will find that you have excluded life itself.[10]

Humans also can have very unpleasant encounters with animals or plants, the results of which can lead to serious illness or death. Many plants and animals need these defences to survive in the world. Eliminating them to make life easier for humans could make the plants and animals more susceptible to danger and possible extinction. Although the Bible may indicate that all animals and plants were provided for the benefit of humankind, this does not imply that they do not have the right to defend themselves.

The final part of this initial argument relates to humans themselves. I suggested earlier that we could change our behaviour so that we lived together without any unpleasantness, but is this really possible? In the Garden of Eden there were two humans. Adam and Eve needed no house. Their food was provided. Could millions of humans really coexist in complete harmony?

Today, mundane tasks, which may be regarded as unpleasant, such as washing dishes, ironing, cleaning toilets and generally keeping the house clean and tidy, have to be carried out in order for the household to function properly. Rubbish disposal and supervising sewerage treatment – two tasks which many would consider to be unpleasant occupations – have to be performed by paid employees in order for society to operate efficiently.

We live in a world of competition. How can two football teams compete for a trophy without one being disappointed? How can golf or tennis tournaments, for example, take place without those not winning being disappointed? Losing is unpleasant.

To sum up this argument, I think it is clear that the idea of living in a world where there is no unpleasantness is almost impossible to entertain. The obstacles appear to be insurmountable, which is why Christians look forward to eternal life.

The desire for a world without unpleasantness

My second argument is very much related to the first. Would we really want to live in a world where there was no unpleasantness?

---

[10] *The Problem of Pain* by C.S. Lewis, p.22

Initially, a form of utopia appears to be very attractive. There would be no financial or health worries. Every activity in which we participated would be pleasurable. We would all co-operate and live in harmony together.

What exactly would we do? All activities are supposedly pleasurable. As mentioned before, could we really find enjoyment in completing the more mundane tasks such as weeding the flowerbeds, washing the dishes or cleaning the toilets? More importantly, would there be any need to think? Exercising the brain is regarded as important, but if everything were provided, how could we use our brains constructively? We have already seen that all forms of competition would be difficult to envisage in this environment. Even games of Patience, where you theoretically play against yourself, would have to result in a successful outcome. This would become predictable and consequently boring.

Businesses employ great minds to discover new and easier ways of doing things, so that they can produce items that are more efficient and cost-effective than those of their competitors. How would new discoveries be made if no one was motivated to search for them? Entertainment usually requires entertainers to become very proficient at a specific skill, whether it be playing a musical instrument or acting. It could be argued that talented musicians enjoy producing music that is of the best quality, but would they really be motivated to attain that standard if there were no other reward?

Would we have to live in similar houses, eat the same food and drive the same cars in order that some people were not seen to be more privileged than others? Would we have to be of equal intelligence or equally good-looking to ensure that no one was disadvantaged? It is not easy to see how everyone can be happy if there are marked differences between people. These differences often produce conflict of sorts. There was one couple in the Garden of Eden. There could be no comparisons. What if there were more people? There would have to be physical differences. In fact, it is interesting to note that as soon as offspring appear in the form of Cain and Abel, there is conflict almost immediately. Granted, conditions had already changed, but it does not take long for one of the sons to initiate unpleasantness. What appears to be the dominant reason for this? Humans have emotions.

What about human emotions in a world where nothing is unpleasant? Falling in love would be easy. We would have to fall in love with one, and only one, person who immediately reciprocated that love. There would be no negative emotions like anger, sorrow, pain, jealousy or greed. This would be an excellent state of affairs, but how could we possibly feel the joy of falling in love without at some stage experiencing the sorrow caused by the death of a loved one? Surely, one of the reasons we experience the positive emotions of joy and happiness is because we can compare these feelings with the negative emotions we experience when faced with pain and sorrow. We need the negative in order to experience the positive. Would we really wish to live in a world without emotions? Kreeft comments in *The Case for Faith* that to love is a choice, but alongside the choice to love is the possibility that people may choose to hate.[11]

From these arguments, it would appear that if it were possible to live in a world without unpleasantness, then such a world would need to be a world without challenges. Perhaps we do not wish to be challenged. God, however, appears to have other ideas. As we will discover with the next two arguments, challenges are critical in our relationship with God.

I hope that most readers by now will realise that a world without unpleasantness is very difficult, if not impossible, to envisage. There remain some aspects of unpleasantness that could be perceived to be unnecessary, one of which is the concept of suffering through illness and disease. I discuss the issue of suffering in more detail in Chapter 5. There may be an argument to suggest that terminal diseases are a way of curbing the increase in population. I would like to point out that if this were the sole reason for illness and disease, God could ensure that those succumbing to terminal illnesses would die without the prolonged suffering that often accompanies them. He could also dispense with all diseases and illnesses if he so wished. No, I think there is another reason that God allows – notice I say allows rather than ordains – suffering, and this brings me to the next two arguments relating to the need for unpleasantness in the world.

The need for God

The first of these poses the question: Would we really need God if there were no unpleasantness?

---

[11] Kreeft in Strobel, p.37

The answer appears to be, no, we probably would not. Humans are most likely to turn to God when they are suffering. When people prosper, with every aspect of their lives seemingly under control, they tend to believe that they do not need God. People are more likely to pray for help rather than thank God for his blessings. Why would God create a world in which he was not needed? As C.S. Lewis says in *The Problem of Pain*:

> *If he who in himself can lack nothing chooses to need us, it is because we need to be needed.*[12]

I believe that God has created a world in which he, quite rightly, wants to be the centre of attention. He has established a set of circumstances where his people need him. Lewis says:

> *While what we call 'our own life' remains agreeable we will not surrender it to him. What then can God do in our own interests but make 'our own life' less agreeable to us, and take away the plausible sources of false happiness?*[13]

God has structured a situation where things happen that cause his people to turn to him for support and guidance. This is not to say that he engineers situations where people suffer. He allows events to unfold and then intervenes when asked. If we lived in a form of utopia, where nothing unpleasant ever happened, would we really spend time thanking God? Why bother, when we know nothing unpleasant will occur?

There is no doubt that some tragedies do turn people away from God. David Watson, in his book *Fear No Evil*, mentions two fathers, both of whom suffered the loss of a child. As a result of the loss, one father, a committed Christian, turned away from God, rejecting him completely. The other, a non-Christian, became a committed Christian. This is a risk that God accepts. He knows that some people who have experienced unpleasantness will never turn to him. That is no fault of God's. God will provide the necessary support if we ask him. We must remember that the greatest tragedy in the history of mankind resulted in the ultimate victory – the crucifixion and resurrection of Jesus.

---

[12] Lewis, p.39
[13] Lewis, p.84

People have the free will to seek or reject this support. We need to realise that God created the world for a purpose. That purpose was to manufacture an environment where he is the centre of attention. Nobody creates anything that serves no purpose. Why would God create a world in which the principal beings of his creation could live without him? Perhaps if more of those who were suffering thought more carefully about the whole concept of unpleasantness and why it exists, they might turn to him more readily and there would be a significant increase in the number of Christians.

I hasten to add that God does not enjoy watching his people suffer. His desire is to assist all those who suffer and to ease that suffering as quickly as possible, but he must be asked to do so. He delights in the pleasure of relieving suffering. He is there to help under all circumstances.

Unpleasantness makes us stronger

My last argument is that God uses our suffering to make us stronger and, consequently, better Christians. In *The Case for Faith*, one of the experts with whom Lee Strobel is discussing the concept of evil and suffering points out that certain attributes, for example courage, would be impossible if there were no pain or suffering. As Paul states, Romans 5:3-4, "Suffering produces perseverance; perseverance character; and character hope."

R.T. Kendall has written a very useful book called *The Thorn in the Flesh*, in which he suggests that God allows us to have a thorn in the flesh because this will lead us to a more meaningful relationship with him. I will discuss the issue of tests and temptations in Chapter 7, but there are several passages in the Bible where it appears that God wants to test his people so that we do in fact become better Christians. However, as Paul states in 1 Corinthians 10:13, God will always ensure that no test will be too severe for the individual to endure. God will always provide a means of overcoming the test. Both James 1:2 and 1 Peter 1:6-7 indicate that as Christians we should be glad when we undergo trials because these trials will make us stronger. R.T. Kendall, in his book *Pure Joy*, describes the joy that can be experienced when undergoing trials. It is a difficult concept to understand. Most people associate joy with happiness. We experience joy when events are working in our favour, for example falling in love, financial gain or sporting success. This, though, is superficial joy that lasts for a finite period of time. The joy experienced when overcoming trials and being closer to God is far deeper and outlasts any superficial joy.

Paul and Silas sang hymns when they were imprisoned (Acts 16:24). Richard Wurmbrand (*Tortured for Christ*) sang hymns when he was imprisoned. Others who experienced joy in their sufferings were Corrie ten Boom and her sister, Betsy (*The Hiding Place*), Brother Yun (*The Heavenly Man*) and Darlene Deibler Rose (*Evidence Not Seen*). These people experienced incredible hardships, but their faith increased as the situation worsened, and their sufferings brought them closer to God.

It may seem odd, but it does appear that there is a special form of joy that can be experienced by overcoming tests or trials. None of this would be possible in a world without unpleasantness. It is suggested that in fact the typical Christian comes from a developing country and lives under the continual danger of persecution.[14]

Free will and evil

Having considered four arguments as to why God permits the presence of evil in his world, I would now like to discuss the connection between free will and evil.

As pointed out in Chapter 1, free will implies choice. Simple choices such as deciding what to wear have little impact on anyone else. However, other decisions will inevitably affect someone adversely, for example deciding to use the supermarket rather than the local shop. Those suffering as a result of your decision will be experiencing some degree of unpleasantness. This may even be true when you are attempting to be generous, as is illustrated by the following scenario.

You find that you have a spare £100 and decide to give it to Charity A. Just before you make the donation, you watch an appeal on television and decide that you wish to support the appeal. You make a decision to split your donation so that half goes to Charity A and half to the television appeal. Both organisations thank you for your donation. Charity A may never realise that it has in fact been disadvantaged when you changed your mind. It has now received £50 less than it would have done, as a result of which some sort of distribution of its funds will be affected.

---

[14] Neff in Strobel, p.209

The example may appear trivial, but it illustrates the concept that freedom of choice will often affect someone adversely.

Comparatively minor choices, for example deciding what to eat, can have profound effects on others. We may decide to eat meat, thereby supporting farmers. Conversely, we may decide to be vegetarian because we consider the farming and killing of animals for human consumption to be wrong. Each of these decisions has its supporters and opponents. Those against any decision will often regard that point of view to be wrong and may in some cases suggest that it is evil.

Celebrities can have a profound effect on the sales of various brands by deciding which to promote. These choices can be worth vast sums of money to the various manufacturers. Members of the royal family can inadvertently start a trend in clothing. When the young Prince George was photographed in a nautical romper suit, sales of this particular item skyrocketed.

In some cases, the effect of our decision can be catastrophic, particularly if it involves a particular person directly, as may be the case when considering long-term relationships with others. One half of a partnership can be devastated if their partner decides to terminate the relationship.

It is not only individuals or groups of people that may be affected by our decisions. Each time we decide to drive our car, pollution is added to the atmosphere.

Even if every decision we make is made for all the right reasons, in making it, other possible choices will have been rejected because there was an element of comparative negativity that has made them unacceptable. Undoubtedly, negativity or unpleasantness has to exist in order for us to make decisions. Often we hear that a decision has been made because it is the "lesser of two evils". I do not think I have heard the opposite, for example, that a decision has been made because it is the "greater of two goods". If God wishes his people to have free will, there must be the opportunity to differentiate between choices on the basis of merit. That can only be done if we can perceive the possible negative effects in certain choices. If there was no unpleasantness, there would be no basis upon which to make our decisions. When God created human beings with free will, he presented them with a choice regarding wrongdoing. Therefore, there was always the chance that evil, and consequently suffering, would result.

Even though God has permitted the presence of evil in his world, it is important to be reminded that in many cases it is decisions made by human beings that have initiated it. As C.S. Lewis says in *The Problem of Pain*:

> *When souls become wicked they will use [pain] to hurt one another; and this perhaps accounts for four-fifths of the sufferings of men. It is men, not God, who have produced racks, whips, prisons, slavery, guns, bayonets and bombs; it is by the churlishness of nature, that we have poverty and overwork.*[15]

Again, Kreeft believes that most of the pain in the world is caused by our choices to be selfish, irresponsible, break our promises, disparage, stray sexually and kill.[16]

In conclusion, it would appear that God created a world in which he knew there would be unpleasantness. He could have created an ideal environment in which everything was good – and he may well have done with the Garden of Eden. However, God decided that he wished to give humans the freedom to accept or reject him as Lord. In order to do this, God gave humans free will to think for themselves and do what they wished. Richard Swinburne, in Peter Williams' book *The Case for God*, says:

> *The possibility of humans bringing about significant evil is a logical consequence of their having ... free and responsible choice. Not even God could give us this choice without the possibility of resulting evil.*[17]

God has engineered circumstances so that at any time his people can turn to him and ask for help and guidance. God has designed a situation where he is needed. In order for this to work satisfactorily, there has to be good and evil. Humans have to have the option to carry out deeds that are contrary to God's will and are therefore unpleasant. However, God's people come closer to him through trials.

The only way to prevent evil is to remove freedom of choice, which would effectively reduce human beings to puppets.

---

[15] Lewis, p.77
[16] Kreeft in Strobel, p.38
[17] Swinburne in *The Case for God* by Peter S. Williams, p.66

I hope I have convinced you that, unfortunately, unpleasantness is necessary in this world. This leads to another very important question that is often asked by both Christians and non-Christians:

How does God, who is good, manage to oversee a world in which there is unpleasantness?

The allocation of evil

God has allocated everything unpleasant to an adversary – Satan. I do not believe it is necessary to speculate as to Satan's origins or characteristics. It is sufficient to point out that, although very powerful, Satan is less powerful than God. Although Satan is responsible for every unpleasantness in the world, it must be remembered that God has ultimate control. At any time God can intervene to prevent any unpleasant deed if he so wishes. Christians can therefore credit God as being responsible for every good event and Satan as being responsible for all that is unpleasant.

People are more ready to accept God as being associated with good, than they are to accept Satan as being associated with evil. Despite this obvious delineation of responsibilities, God is still blamed for both good and bad! If anyone questions God's decisions regarding evil, we can always quote John 3:16: "For God so loved the world that he gave his one and only son, that whoever believes in him shall not perish but have eternal life."

In *The Case for God*, Hugh Silvester is quoted as saying, "God has done everything possible, short of un-making man and depriving him of his free will."[18] Through sending his son, Jesus, to die for our sins, God has put in motion a series of events that will eventually see Satan and all unpleasantness defeated. Good will eventually prevail. Meanwhile, humans have the free will to follow a path that is either unpleasant or good, without or with God.

C.T. Studd once said:

> *Christ came to save us by his blood and by his Spirit; blood to wash away our past sins, Spirit to change our hearts and empower us to live right. He came not to save us* in *our sins but* from *them.*

---

[18] Silvester in Williams, p.73

He went on to say that people...

> *...need to see hell as the result of their sin, and that produces fear, the fear of God which is the beginning of wisdom.*[19]

These are strong words, but perhaps we need to use our free will to look more closely at what God really expects of us. It is we who need to change and not God. All too often we question God, so in the next chapter I will consider why God sometimes chooses to intervene and why at other times he does not.

---

[19] *C.T. Studd, Cricketer and Pioneer* by N.P. Grubb, pp. 206, 207

CHAPTER FIVE

God and Intervention

As we have already seen, God has given the people of this world free will. They can do what they like, when they like and how they like. If God had decided to impose his will on everybody, because he is good, we would live in a perfect world. Nothing would go wrong. No one would be hungry. There would be no disease and no disasters. We anticipate such a situation when we inherit eternal life and meet God. A "perfect" world sounds ideal but, as was pointed out in the previous chapter, there are reasons why such a state of affairs does not exist and God has permitted evil. This ensures that humans have free will. God obviously knew that given this unbounded freedom, humans would misuse this power, so there are times when he has to intervene. Some people believe that he never intervenes. Many believe that perhaps he does intervene on occasions, but wonder why he does not do so more often.

My first response is that in all probability God intervenes more often than we realise. Unfortunately, the majority of his interventions go unnoticed. People more readily highlight those occasions when God appears to have allowed events that can be seen as evil or unnecessary to have taken place without intervening.

In this chapter I consider particular situations in which God is blamed for non-intervention and suggest possible reasons for his inaction. I also describe events and circumstances where he does appear to have intervened, but his actions have often been largely unnoticed.

Why doesn't God intervene to prevent tragedies?

God's ultimate desire is to give every human the opportunity to make the decision to follow him and become a Christian. In order to make that decision we must have free will, but equally we must also have the opportunity to reject him. That is the risk God takes. God has given every individual the free will to make the one decision that, above every other decision, matters most. We must understand, though, that by allowing humans to have free will God cannot intervene on a regular basis. Although God will always assist his followers when asked, generally he will not interfere. It is the failure to comprehend the implications of this that leads to misdirected blame. As C.S. Lewis explains in *The Problem of Pain:*

> *A world ... continually underpropped and corrected by divine interference, would have been a world in which nothing important ever depended on human choice.*[20]

When certain tragedies that are perceived to be avoidable occur, God is blamed for not intervening. Despite the arguments already mentioned regarding free will and the existence of evil, surely, if God is good, he could intervene more often to prevent seemingly pointless tragedies from occurring.

Perhaps one of the most tragic occurrences is the premature death of a child. Time after time parents will ask, "Why, if God exists and is good, does he allow the death of a child?" My response is that although God knows in advance that a certain child is about to die, he never under any circumstances ordains it. As I have explained previously, I believe that God never demands the death of any individual to suit his purposes. We know that God has advance knowledge of the event and we know that he can intervene to prevent any tragedy he wishes. So why does he let it happen?

Before going further, let us consider two scenarios. The first involves three principal characters: the father of one family (Mr A), the mother of another (Mrs B) and a milkman.

Mr A is married with a young family. One day he has to travel to London for a very important interview for a new job. As he is getting dressed, his youngest child, a baby of three months, wakes and starts

---

[20] Lewis, p.59

crying. Mrs A appears to be sleeping after a rather disturbed night. Mr A decides that he can probably feed and change the baby's nappy without bothering his wife and it should still leave him enough time to get to the station to catch the train. Unfortunately, the task takes more time than he anticipated, and so when he gets into the car he is worried about missing the train.

Meanwhile, in the next village the milkman has delivered the milk to Mrs B's house. Unfortunately, when he closed the gate at the end of her path, the latch didn't engage, so the gate has swung open in the breeze.

Mrs B also has young children, one aged twelve months and one nearly two and a half. She is wearing her dressing-gown as she wakes the two children and gives them breakfast. She then opens the front door and collects the milk. At that moment there is a scream from the kitchen. Mrs B turns round and hurries inside. With the milk in one hand, she shuts the front door with the other. As with the gate, it does not engage the latch and swings open in the breeze. Once in the kitchen she scolds the older child who has knocked the younger one's bowl onto the floor. While Mrs B clears up the mess, the older child runs into the hall and through the open front door. He sees a cat sunning itself on the wall across the road.

At the same time, Mr A is driving through the village a little over the speed limit, as he is trying to make up time to catch his train. He, too, notices the cat on the side of the road. He assesses that it is sufficiently sleepy that it won't suddenly leave the wall and run across the road, but he keeps an eye on it. With his line of vision on the other side of the road, partially obscured by parked cars, he fails to notice Mrs B's older child who is now running down the path and out through the open gate. The child runs across the road and is killed instantly by Mr A's car.

The lives of all those involved and their families are changed for ever. Although the milkman may not realise immediately that it was he who left the gate open, he could eventually conclude that he was partially to blame. The effect on Mrs B's family is obvious. Not only will she probably attach some blame to Mr A (and possibly the milkman) but she will also have realised that the accident would never have happened had she closed the door securely. Despite having no realistic chance of avoiding the child, Mr A was exceeding the speed limit and was not fully concentrating on the road. In all probability, he will receive a conviction for dangerous driving with a custodial sentence. This could well have long-term effects on his family, emotionally and financially.

All three characters, but particularly Mr A and Mrs B, if counselled by someone from the local church, would question why, if he exists, God did not intervene to prevent the horrendous accident. He could have done so at several key stages in the scenario but apparently chose not to – a decision that changed the lives of the characters and their families for ever. For many people, sometimes both Christians and non-Christians, it is hard to understand why, if God is good and all-powerful, he appears to be content to allow tragedies to happen.

Consider a second scenario. A young mother living in a drought-affected part of Africa has been trying to find food for her only child who is the same age as the one killed in the first scenario. The child becomes weaker and weaker, eventually dying before the mother can find the necessary food. This scenario happens more often than the first, but rarely attracts the same attention. Before considering why God has not intervened in either of these scenarios, we need to pause to understand that in God's eyes the two children who have died are of equal importance. Too often in today's world, the first scenario is seen as a tragedy, whereas the second is seen as merely a fact of life. Often lives of certain individuals are perceived to be of greater value than others.

Although God could intervene every time a child was about to die, why does he not do so? It is probably useful to respond to this question by first considering the ramifications if God did decide to intervene on a more regular basis. I believe the answer lies in the implications of his constant intervention. If he did intervene every time a child was about to die, what would be the consequences? The first point relates to the question, when is a child not a child, i.e. when does God stop intervening because the child is no longer a child? Should he intervene for every child under the age of 12, 14, 16 or 18? Where is he to set the limit? If there is no limit, then he will be intervening every time someone is about to die prematurely. This raises the additional question of what is considered premature death, given that life expectancy is on the rise.

If God were to protect all children from accidents, diseases, etc., they would then become suddenly susceptible to them at a specific age when they were no longer protected. If children knew that they were safe from accidental death, then how would they learn to act responsibly on the road, in the school or at home? Children have to be prepared for life. They have to be exposed to danger so that they recognise it. Unfortunately, this means that some children will die prematurely. Similarly, they need to be aware of health problems and how to live healthy lives. It is all part of the learning process. Society takes more and more steps to ensure the safety of its children. In fact, some people now worry that perhaps we have become over-cautious, to the extent that children grow up being less aware of the dangers around them because they are never exposed to the risks that exist.

People often ask, "Why does God allow children to be born with disabilities?" Unfortunately, certain members of society will provide very unhelpful answers. It has been suggested that the Bible states that the sins of certain members of the family cause members of the next generation to be born with disabilities as some sort of family punishment. However, why should God, if he is good, require an innocent person to suffer on behalf of a guilty person? This seems a very strange idea. In Exodus 20:5, part of the second commandment does suggest that children may be punished because of the sins of their fathers. I believe this possibly relates to the circumstances in which the children may find themselves as a result of their father's actions. For example, children of a man who has lost his money through foolish decisions will inevitably suffer as a result. I do not believe that God seeks out the children of sinful fathers and punishes those children for their father's actions.

Others will suggest that God selects special families to have disabled children, and that these families should feel honoured that God has selected them to look after a "special" child. Again, I reiterate that God does not cause suffering in a particular person to make others feel privileged. I believe the situation is similar to that regarding the death of a child. God does not cause disabilities. He knows a disabled child is about to be born and he will, when asked, help the family support that child in every way possible.

Certain disabilities are more serious than others. If God were to eradicate all mental or physical disorders that are currently regarded as disabilities, other aspects of the child would suddenly become disabilities. Parents would question the reason behind their child being born inferior in looks, intelligence or even sporting prowess. Unintelligent or less able children, in particular, would be regarded as having a disability. Because disabilities are relative, as soon as the more severe ones were eradicated others would emerge. The eradication of all "disabilities" would only occur if all humans were born identical!

There are ways that some disabilities can be eradicated. Some deformities in children have been caused by the mother's behaviour during the pregnancy, for example, excessive smoking. Others have occurred due to the administration of certain drugs, for example thalidomide, which was mentioned previously. It may be that in the future, scientists will discover other factors that lead to certain disabilities, resulting in their eradication. If asked, God will assist in all areas of medical research.

Why does God allow natural disasters and atrocities to happen?

In Chapter 4, I suggested that some natural disasters are caused by humans attempting to interfere with nature. I believe that some catastrophes are predictable. For example, if we build houses on flood plains, why are we surprised when the inhabitants are devastated by floods? If we live in areas prone to earthquakes, why are we surprised when the area is subjected to a serious earthquake? If we destroy vast areas of forest, why are we surprised by the advent of droughts? Some disasters do appear to be more random, but may still have been caused by the actions of humans. Much remains to be learnt about the weather. It may well be that certain meteorological conditions, which at the moment appear to be random, are actually caused by the actions of humans somewhere on the planet.

Until the middle of the twentieth century, it was believed that there was order to everything. There was then the emergence of Chaos Theory, which demonstrates the random nature of events. In one of the early discussions on the theory, it was suggested that the flapping of a butterfly's wings in one country could initiate a chain of events that may lead to a hurricane in another country. As humans, we do not fully understand the consequences of our actions or decisions. When an earthquake or tsunami occurs, there appears to be little or no association with any specific action taken by humans, but maybe in time scientists will discover links. At present, such events are often referred to as "acts of God", which I believe to be very unfair on God. The message from God appears to be that humans have the resources to prepare for these catastrophes, and in the case of some, for example the tsunamis, warning systems can be put in place to minimise the loss of life.

This may help explain why God allows natural disasters to occur without warning, especially if they do in fact result from human actions. As with children, we need to learn that there are risks associated with certain actions or decisions. God will not intervene every time a mistake is made, or we will never learn from these mistakes. It is not God's fault that houses have been built on flood plains, without adequate protection. Instead, we have to develop techniques to predict when disasters may occur and take the necessary precautions. In addition, as will be discussed further in the next chapter, God is not some sort of "fairy godmother" who waves a magic wand every time there is a problem!

God should not be blamed for atrocities that occur as a direct result of malicious human actions. I have heard people suggest that God should have intervened with the Holocaust. The Holocaust was not the fault of God. He has given us free will, and therefore, if a particular section of society decides to do something abhorrent, God does not have an obligation to intervene. The responsibility lies with other societies or nations to ensure that similar events do not recur. Incidentally, similar atrocities have continued to occur in the form of ethnic cleansing. It is the role of other nations to intervene and put procedures in place to prevent future occurrences. All too often, there are "diplomatic" reasons why countries are left to their own devices. The argument remains the same. If God were to intervene on a regular basis at one particular level, then where would he stop? Someone will always point out that he should be intervening at the next level. At times, God does intervene on behalf of individuals who are being persecuted under some regime, but only if he has been asked. There will be more regarding God's intervention in tragedies of all kinds as a response to prayer which I consider in the next chapter.

Why does God allow pain and suffering?

Physical pain is another form of suffering which is perceived to be unnecessary. We have the means to alleviate pain through the administration of painkillers, but often these bring only temporary relief. Many people suffer from illnesses and diseases, some more painful than others. Why should people suffer in this way? Those who suffer from debilitating illnesses or find themselves in other circumstances of prolonged pain wonder why God allows them to suffer. These situations may be evil but they cannot be attributed to God. He cannot intervene each time someone is suffering, for reasons similar to those given as to why he does not always intervene when children are about to die. Suffering is relative. If God is to intervene consistently, at what level of suffering should he intervene?

As Denis Alexander points out in his book *Creation or Evolution*,[21] pain is actually essential for the wellbeing of most, if not all, species in the animal kingdom. He cites an example of a Pakistani boy who could feel no pain. The boy managed to stab himself and walk on hot coals without feeling the pain. He eventually died after falling from a height, whilst in his early teens. By not being able to react to pain, he had been exposing his body to unnatural acts. If we hold our hand over a flame, we will withdraw it before it is burnt, because of the pain caused by the heat. Physical pain is necessary to provide warning that the body is in danger. Unfortunately, the nervous system is such that pain will persist in circumstances where the body is being attacked but nothing can actually be done to relieve the pain. This is the case with certain diseases and illnesses. Although painkillers can help relieve such pain, the nervous system continues to register the fact that all is not well. At times such as these, prayer, asking God to intervene to alleviate the pain, may be the only solution.

Pain has been used, and still is in some countries, as a form of punishment, supposedly as a deterrent. The rationale has been that if the punishment is sufficiently painful, it will deter people from committing the offence. Unfortunately, there is always a chance that the culprit will evade detection, and so often the gains from the offence are such that the offender is willing to risk the painful punishment. If a misdemeanour had always resulted in a painful consequence, the punishment may well have had a greater chance of success. It is interesting watching animals with electric fences. Sheep, cattle and even, at times, dogs quickly understand the result of touching an electric fence and, consequently, stay away from them no matter what the temptations on the other side!

Suffice it to say, it is difficult to understand how God could intervene on a regular basis in any situation that may be deemed

---

[21] *Creation or Evolution* by Denis Alexander

unpleasant. His intervention has to remain unpredictable in order that humans can exercise their free will and that God does not become some sort of "fairy godmother" who is available on request. As Peter Williams says in his book *The Case for God*:

> *It is no more coincidence that many of the greatest 'saints' have been men and women well acquainted with suffering. God is concerned with our happiness, but he is much more concerned with our wholeness ... Sometimes the unhappiness of suffering is our path to greater wholeness.*[22]

God's intervention

So far in this chapter, I have considered the negative aspects of God's apparent failure to intervene. It is time to focus on the positive. There are times when God most certainly does intervene. In fact, as I stated at the beginning of the chapter, it is probable that he intervenes in a positive way more times than we actually realise.

When the Boxing Day tsunami hit some years ago, many thousands of people lost their lives. Questions were asked regarding God's intervention. One young girl had been studying tsunamis in her class a few weeks earlier. Her teacher had told the class that before any tidal wave arrived, the sea would be sucked from the beach. On the day of the tsunami, the young girl was on the beach on holiday when she noticed the sea receding from the beach. She was therefore able to warn people of what was about to happen and consequently lives were saved. When this story was recounted, there was no suggestion that God might have intervened through the geography lesson. We may be quick to blame him for allowing tragedies to take place, but we are equally slow at acknowledging the possible forewarning of disasters. On many occasions, we are unaware of those interventions because we take things for granted.

Let us return to the scenario where the young boy is killed by the car and consider three alternative outcomes. In the first outcome, the milkman has closed the gate and so when the boy runs out of the house he does not reach the road. The accident never happens. Rushing out of the house behind the boy, Mrs B may breathe a sigh of relief and consider it "lucky" that the gate is closed. If she is a Christian, she

---

[22] Williams, p.71

might say a quick, "Thank you, Lord," but even with Christians this may not happen! The fact is, it is most likely that the event is quickly forgotten.

In the second outcome, Mrs B has closed the front door and so the boy never leaves the house. In this outcome, it is most unlikely that Mrs B will ever have been aware of what could have happened had she not closed the door. The event is likely to be forgotten even more quickly than in the previous scenario. It is highly unlikely that, whether a Christian or not, Mrs B considers the notion that God may well have intervened to save the child.

In the third outcome, the boy rushes out of the house but Mr A notices him and manages to stop his car in time. Mrs B sees the car stop. She thanks Mr A for his quick reactions and leads the young boy back into the house. It just happens that Mrs B's neighbour who is a Christian has witnessed the whole scenario so she tells the vicar what happened. The vicar decides to visit Mrs B who is not a Christian and give thanks for the safe deliverance of the boy from potential disaster. He arrives at the house and this is the conversation that ensues:

"I hear that your son has just had a miraculous escape," the vicar says.

"Yes, indeed," Mrs B replies. "He was so lucky that the driver saw him in time."

"Let us thank God for intervening and saving your son," the vicar suggests.

"It was nothing to do with God," Mrs B says. "I spoke to the driver and thanked him for reacting so quickly. He said it was just lucky that he had managed to stop in time."

Non-Christians believe that narrow escapes can be attributed solely to good fortune and it is very difficult to convince them that God may have in fact played an important role. It is also interesting to anticipate the different reactions from the media. If the driver kills the child, there is no doubt that the story would at least make the headlines in the local paper:

Child Killed by Speeding Driver

If the child were to have been saved because the milkman had closed the gate securely, I doubt very much that the headline in the local paper would have read:

Child Saved by Conscientious Milkman

Of course, the headline would never be:

Child Saved by God

People are quick to sensationalise tragedy, often attributing the blame to God's non-intervention, but are reluctant to credit him when disasters are averted.

One year in the autumn, the area in which I live was hit by a severe storm. We were very fortunate not to lose our power. I didn't thank God for this and in all probability few others, if anyone, thanked him. Two days before Christmas, we had another severe storm and this time the power was affected. This disrupted many of the preparations for Christmas dinner, as many houses were without power for some time. I wonder how many people were asking why God allowed this to happen over Christmas when people were preparing to celebrate the birth of his Son. Perhaps God has a sense of humour and was reminding us that we should have acknowledged his intervention in the first storm!

Why are we so slow to recognise God's hand in the prevention of disasters when they fail to materialise, and yet are so quick to blame him when they happen? I believe it is because we take so much for granted. For example, we expect to be able to get into our cars and drive to work every day without having an accident. It is unlikely that anyone, Christian or non-Christian, will thank God for every safe journey on a day-to-day basis. Christians do in some countries! I have been involved with a community overseas which is based in a very isolated part of the world. Each time we set off on a journey of any significant distance by vehicle, bearing in mind these journeys could be particularly hazardous for any number of reasons, we always prayed for a safe journey.

If we are involved in an accident, especially if the consequences are serious, we may then begin to question God as to why he allowed it to happen. People spend more time questioning God about tragedies than thanking him for normalities.

In general, God has decided that humans will have free will and so he will not intervene as a matter of course, as we have seen earlier in the chapter. When he decides otherwise, there is often a very good reason. One of the most famous of these interventions concerned Saul on the road to Damascus. God decided he wanted to use this man, and the only way to persuade Saul that he was required for a special mission was by dramatic intervention. As we know, the change in Saul's life was profound.

God's intervention in lives today

The question then arises as to how God intervenes in the lives of people today. There are many Christians whose belief in God has been initiated as a result of some sort of intervention by God; their lives have been dramatically altered by this intervention. Sometimes his intervention appears to be very obvious, whereas at other times it may be less so. It is not always crystal-clear whether or not something has taken place by chance.

In Chapter 2, I shared an example of what I believe to have been a very important intervention by God in my life. There have been numerous other such events, many of which have been comparatively trivial but have served to alert me to his presence.

One such event is worth sharing, as the sequence of events was remarkable.

I was visiting friends, which necessitated a journey on the motorway. I arrived at their house on the Friday evening, and as I entered their drive, the bulb in my offside dipped headlight blew. I was due to travel back the following evening in the dark and I was slightly concerned, as I would need the dipped headlights on the motorway; but I felt there was little I could do as I had no idea where to find a garage that might be open on a Saturday. Their house was not close to any major town.

We had planned an all-day activity the following day, so I was anxious to walk my dog and purchase a newspaper before doing the activity. For various reasons I could not walk the dog on or near the property at which I was staying. It was suggested that I should drive to a suitable location a short distance away to walk the dog and then drive on to the neighbouring village where I could buy a paper. As it happened, there was a small garage there where I might be able to purchase a bulb.

So the next morning I drove to the spot and walked the dog. Afterwards, I went to the village and bought a newspaper while the new bulb was being fitted at the garage. I then went to start the car... Nothing. The battery was completely dead. The garage ordered a new battery. I had to leave the car where it was. A lift back to my friends ensured I could do the planned activities and I collected the car later. All was well, but there could have been some dire scenarios if the battery had failed at any other time. If the battery had failed when I restarted the car after walking my dog, I would have been stranded. If I had managed to start the car on one more occasion before the battery had failed, this would have left me stranded at my friend's house in the evening and unable to make the journey home. As it happened, the battery failed in the most convenient place at the right time. Not only that, but also the headlight bulb had blown at just the right time to ensure no inconvenience on the motorway and ensuring that I was at the garage when the battery failed. I believe the sequence of events demonstrated that God was looking after me. It may be something small, but to me it was important.

I think it again useful to consider different scenarios to illustrate ways in which God may choose to intervene. In each case, Mr C is driving to the station to catch the train to work. He is a regular commuter, but on this particular day he needs to be in the office for a vital meeting. Unfortunately, he has left home a little late and is in danger of missing the train.

In the first scenario, he is driving along the road when a tractor pulls out in front of his car. The road has many bends and it is a while before he can overtake safely. He now realises that he will not arrive at the station in time to catch the train and so becomes extremely agitated. When he eventually reaches the station, he finds that the train has been delayed by ten minutes and he will be able to catch it and still arrive in time for his appointment.

The second scenario is identical except that Mr C misses the train and fails to get to the meeting, which proves disastrous for his business.

In the third scenario, events unfold in exactly the same way as in the second scenario, however, the train is involved in a horrendous train crash. Most commuters have regular seats on these trains. It turns out that if Mr C had been sitting in his usual seat, he would almost certainly have been killed.

Although it is not possible to ascertain how big a part God actually played in any of these scenarios, it is possible to consider the reactions of Mr C depending upon whether or not he is a Christian.

Let us consider the three scenarios given that Mr C is a Christian.

He may well look at the first scenario and conclude that God is testing him. It could be a lesson in trust. The fact that the tractor has caused a delay is actually countered by the train being late. As Christians, we often think that a disruptive sequence of events has eventuated simply to annoy us, whereas in fact God may well be using them to test our faith in him. He can intervene at any stage to ensure a favourable outcome.

In the second scenario, all does appear to have been lost, but God may well be using the situation to demonstrate that good can come from a disaster. The right response from Mr C in this scenario would be to pray for God's help in ensuring that there is a favourable long-term outcome. I know of someone who was desperate to marry a particular young lady, but it did not happen. A year or two later he met another young lady, whom he later married very happily. He was delighted to have been given the opportunity to meet and marry this person, as they remained happily married until he died. He was convinced that God played a part in the outcome.

In the third scenario, Mr C would almost certainly have put the outcome down to God's intervention. In fact, he may well have believed that the outcome demonstrated that God had a particular reason for ensuring that he missed the train, because Mr C's outlook on life would have changed utterly.

If Mr C were not a Christian, he may well have put the first two scenarios down to good luck and bad luck respectively and think no more about it. In the third scenario, his attitude could have been very different – he would have considered himself to have been very lucky. The incident may have had a profound effect and assisted him in reconsidering his views concerning God, leading him to the point where he decided to follow God and become a Christian.

God does intervene in the most dramatic of ways, but this is not the norm unless he has a specific agenda, as with the conversion of Paul. God may decide that a dramatic event is required to convert a certain person. In general, people become Christians because they attend events or services and are moved by specific aspects of the preaching. Some people gradually become Christians and cannot point to any dynamic experience.

In this chapter I have endeavoured to explain why I believe that God cannot intervene each time that a tragedy is about to occur. I have also tried to demonstrate that he probably intervenes on more occasions than we realise. Although it is often not possible to say for sure whether or not there was divine intervention in any particular set of events, it is often possible to believe that there was. When discussing prayer in the next chapter, we will see that apparent intervention from God is most likely after prayer.

Free Will

CHAPTER SIX

God and Prayer

The predominant way that a Christian communicates with God is through prayer and God's principal response to our commitment to him and the Christian way of life is through answering prayer. Prayer is about developing a relationship with God. There are many aspects surrounding the concept of prayer, and excellent books have been written on the subject. In this chapter I focus solely on the petitioning aspect of prayer.

When discussing God's omniscience in Chapter 3, we saw that God answers *all* prayer, but not necessarily in the way that we would like or expect. In the words of C.S. Lewis:

> *Whether we like it or not, God intends to give us what we need, not what we think we want.*[23]

How does God answer prayer?

God asks us to pray and he has promised that all prayers will be answered. However, the Christian has no idea exactly how this may happen. The Bible tells us that God will answer prayer: "Therefore I tell you, whatever you ask for in prayer, believe that you have received it, and it will be yours" (Mark 11:24). The Bible also states in 1 John 5:14: "If we ask anything according to his [God's] will, he hears us." Prayers are answered in such a way that the person praying benefits from his response in the way that God thinks most appropriate. His response may be "yes, immediately", "yes, later on", "yes, but not as you are

---

[23] Lewis, p.41

expecting" or "no". Sometimes, his answer may appear to be negative at the time, but later, upon reflection, can often be recognised as being positive.

"Yes, immediately"

The most spectacular responses are often the "yes, immediately" ones. Examples of these are often referred to as miracles, the most obvious of which are generally associated with healing. Someone prays for healing and that healing takes place immediately. It is very hard to understand why miracles happen after some prayers but not after others.

Other dramatic responses to prayer can be seen in the lives of well-known Christians. Brother Andrew tells, in his book *God's Smuggler*, of how he was involved in the distribution of bibles within countries that were at that time behind The Iron Curtain. He tells of one occasion when, having a car stacked with boxes of bibles, he was waiting at a checkpoint to enter one of these countries. The guards were taking a considerable time meticulously searching each car as it approached the checkpoint. Brother Andrew prayed that something would happen to enable him to pass through the checkpoint without the bibles being confiscated. When he reached the front of the queue, the guard checked and stamped Brother Andrew's papers but never even glanced at the contents of the car. When asked, God can answer prayers in spectacular fashion. Unfortunately, many people are under the misapprehension that God should answer *all* prayers in this manner.

"Yes, but later on"

The second response is the "yes, but later on". In the next chapter, I discuss ways in which God may test his followers. The "yes, but later on" may well relate to a specific test that God is using to strengthen the faith of the individual. Delayed response to prayer is a means God uses of developing our trust in him. He knows our needs and will often intervene at the last moment, showing that he is in control. This is particularly relevant when seeking financial help. In Christian literature, we often read of churches that have received financial assistance at the very last minute, often with funds emanating from a completely unexpected source. If God supports an appeal he will not let it fail, but he may well test the faith of the congregation in the process.

There are Christian pastors who rely entirely on contributions from their congregation to support not only their ministry but also their living. At times, the situation is critical when the donation suddenly arrives. C.T. Studd tells of the time when he and his family were missionaries overseas, relying entirely upon money sent from the United Kingdom. On one occasion, they were particularly desperate. The postbag arrived – not a very regular occurrence! He and his wife emptied it and opened the various letters. There was plenty of news from family and friends but not a single penny pledged from anyone. They had no idea what to do. Their young family needed feeding. They decided to look in the bag once more. One letter had become lodged in the mesh of the bag. They opened it. It contained £100, which was more than enough to keep them going until the next postbag arrived.

More examples of instances where God appears to have withheld aid until the last minute can be found in the book *Nevertheless* by John Kirkby. This book looks at the origins of Christians Against Poverty. Time after time money was required to meet commitments. Often it seemed that the situation was hopeless. Yet God never failed to respond, always providing what was needed to continue the work of the organisation, even if it was at the very last moment. God is showing that he will not abandon those who trust in him, but he expects absolute trust. Help will arrive in time but no earlier!

Other books that merit reading if you wish to see evidence of answered prayers include Clive Langmead's *Robber of the Cruel Streets*, which recounts the story of George Müller, Isobel Kuhn's *By Searching* and Brother Andrew's *God's Smuggler*, from which I related a story earlier. There are instances in each of these books of God's intervention, often at the last moment.

An amusing but poignant story from Brother Andrew is worth recounting here. He tells of a time when he desperately needed one shilling to send an item in the post by registered mail (obviously some time ago!). The last day on which the item could be posted to ensure its arrival at its destination on time had arrived. There was a knock at the door and Brother Andrew was confronted by an old friend who was in desperate need of money for some food. As they were talking and Brother Andrew was about to explain that he had nothing to give his friend, he spied a shilling coin in the gravel, which his friend had obviously not noticed. It was just what Brother Andrew needed. He managed to surreptitiously pick up the coin and slide it into his pocket without his friend noticing. Immediately he realised that this was not what God had intended and so he handed the coin to his friend. With possibly the last chance of finding the money to pay the postage for his package, he said goodbye to his friend and turned round to go back inside the house. As he did so, the postman appeared. He had a most unexpected letter for Brother Andrew that contained more than enough money for the posting of the item.

I have had times in my life, particularly when studying, when funds have been exhausted, only to be replenished just in time. On one occasion, I was literally down to my last tin of baked beans when a cheque arrived in the post!

"Yes, but not as you are expecting"

The third type of response is the "yes, but not as you are expecting". I mentioned earlier the young man who appeared to have his hopes of a happy marriage blocked by God only to find that God had a different plan, which ultimately led to greater happiness. This type of response can be very painful at the time but upon reflection later, it becomes obvious that God answers the prayer in the way that is best for the individual in the long term. Job-seeking is another area where Christians often feel that God does not answer prayers in the way that they hope. Not being selected for a particular position, which at that moment in time appears to be most desirable, tests our trust in God. It is only later, upon reflection, that we appreciate that the position was not in our best interests.

This is perhaps one reason why Christians should utilise prayer lists. On that list there will inevitably be prayers that do not appear to have been answered. It is only on reflection, often years later, that we realise that these prayers have been answered but not in the way that we expected.

"No"

The fourth response is the outright "no". There has to be a "no". This is actually similar to the "yes, but not as you are expecting". I am single, and at times I have prayed that I might find a woman to marry and then I could start a family. This request has never been granted. However, without the financial obligations associated with raising a family, I have been able to sponsor students in a developing country through secondary school and university, offering them a future, which until then they had no hope of being realised. God had other plans for me, and my resources. I would never have been able to afford to both support a family and sponsor students in the way that I have done.

We must also realise that we cannot expect God to grant our requests simply because we ask him. As I mentioned in the previous chapter, God is not a "fairy godmother" who grants our every wish. There would be a multitude of lottery winners if every wish to win the lottery were granted! God is not some type of "eternal slot-machine" in which a request is inserted that hits the jackpot every time. Nor should we, as C.S. Lewis quotes a friend as saying, "...regard God as an airman regards his parachute; it is there for emergencies but he hopes he'll never have to use it."[24]

One of the reasons for God's unwillingness to grant our requests is that these wished-for responses may not be in the long-term interests of his people. We also have to remember that we are on this planet for a purpose. We are here to learn to follow God's ways and lead lives that please him. It is his desire that we will become completely faithful to him. For many reasons, few if any Christians attain this goal. Meeting our requests instantly on demand renders the concept of faith meaningless. God desires progress from all his followers. We are to increase our faith in him as we journey through this life. As our faith increases, we will become better people and achieve greater things in his name. Treating God as an eternal "fairy godmother" granting instant requests not only negates the need for faith but also produces a situation that quickly becomes unsustainable and ridiculous.

There has to be an unknown factor, a mystery in the way that God responds to prayers. Not only does that increase the faith that his people have in him, but it also ensures that he can respond in the way that he desires. He is in total control. God wants his people to pray sensibly, earnestly, rationally and persistently, believing that he will respond in a way that he deems to be optimal at the particular time. This may often lead us to experience times of despair, and to feelings of rejection and abandonment, but this is part of the deepening of our faith in God. We need to be tested and challenged. As will be discussed in the next chapter, God tests us to make us stronger. Perseverance is a characteristic that needs to be developed in the individual Christian. It

[24] Lewis, p.84

often takes a lifetime for Christians to learn that God has all the answers and always acts in the best interests of his people.

There are, though, many other very good reasons why some prayers appear to attract a negative response. There are situations where it is impossible, even for God, to answer prayers satisfactorily! Let me qualify this. In Chapter 4, when discussing the concept of evil, I pointed out that competition in a world without unpleasantness would be impossible. All football matches, for example, would have to end as a draw if one team and its supporters were to not to suffer the anguish of losing. There is a similar problem when it comes to the response to prayer. Even though it is a fairly trivial example, let us consider the scenario where two football teams reach the final of an important competition. Neither team has accomplished this feat previously. Both teams may have regarded themselves as lucky to reach the final. A supporter from each of the two teams prays fervently that their team will win this important match. There can, however, be only one winner, and so one of the two supporters cannot have their prayer answered positively. This is a trivial example, and in the greater scheme of things, there are far more important issues than winning football matches. It does, however, highlight the fact that in many cases there are two conflicting requests that cannot both be granted simultaneously. Two people may be applying for the same job, hoping to purchase the same house, or even desiring to marry the same spouse! As I have already shown, God may use initial disappointment to provide a more favourable alternative at a later date.

There are other situations where it is not possible to please all parties due to a conflict of interest. As we know, rain is a necessity when it comes to growing produce, but it can also be a nuisance, particularly in the United Kingdom!

Let us assume that a farmer has just planted his crops and he needs rain in the next few weeks to ensure that they grow properly. Next door to the farmer is a large campsite. This is the busiest time of year and the owner hopes that it will stay dry for the duration of the holidays. Even rain at night could inconvenience or deter visitors. The farmer wants the rain, but the campsite owner does not. Both livelihoods could be affected depending upon the outcome. Theoretically, rain on the farm but not the campsite is possible, but it is most unlikely! The campsite owner might not begrudge the farmer some rain, but would certainly not desire the quantity that the farmer may well need. There are conflicts of interest in many situations. The building of wind turbines, new railways and new houses always highlights a difference of opinions between those in favour of the new project and those against.

We pray for peace in the international sphere, where circumstances are such that the state of affairs appears to be irredeemable, mainly due to historical events initiated by human decisions. In these situations, we often cannot envisage a solution. Perhaps one of the most well-known situations concerns the conflict between the Israelis and the Palestinians, particularly relating to the City of Jerusalem. Without trying to analyse the situation in great detail, both nations feel that the city belongs to them. Although some degree of power-sharing appears to be the only solution, the situation is so complex that even the most enthusiastic peace negotiators are finding a genuine and lasting solution to be almost impossible to attain. I mention this situation again in Chapter 10, because there may be a solution!

A similar situation has been evident in Ireland. There are people, both in Ireland and Northern Ireland, who believe that Ireland should be united as one country and others who believe that Northern Ireland should remain part of the United Kingdom. If the Catholics in the country are praying for one scenario and the Protestants for the alternative, one group will not have its prayers answered satisfactorily. The next best situation is one of compromise, but that is always difficult and may be contrary to what many of those involved believe should happen. God will help, but often humans have used their free will to produce situations so complex that there is no solution that will satisfy everyone.

How should we respond to disappointment?

It is those prayers that appear to be both answerable and justifiable, but appear not to be answered in a positive manner, which cause the most anguish. This is especially true when praying for the healing of other people. There is the well-documented case of the late David Watson, a brilliant Christian minister, who died of cancer at a comparatively young age. Christians could not understand why God apparently did not answer the overwhelming number of prayers for his healing, as David had so much to offer the Christian church. I have experienced a similar disappointment when praying for a friend who died of cancer in her fifties, when she too had so much to offer. To this day, I cannot understand why God did not intervene and provide the necessary healing. As Christians, we hope that we will discover the answers to these questions when we leave this world and move on.

At this stage, it is worth considering in more detail how we, as Christians, respond to situations that end tragically, even though we have prayed. I discussed earlier why God does not prevent all tragedies. I suggested in Chapter 4 reasons why God permits the presence of evil in the world. Tragedies will occur – and at times, it will appear that God has ignored our prayers.

In the previous chapter I introduced the scenario of the child who was killed when running out from the house. Let us consider an alternative outcome to the accident. Suppose that the child had survived the accident but had been very seriously injured. People had then prayed earnestly that God would heal the child, but the child had failed to recover and had died. The immediate reaction may well have been to have questioned the response to the prayers. Why pray if God will not intervene?

However difficult it may be, those involved in a tragic event have to accept that the event has occurred and life has to go on. Questioning or blaming God achieves nothing. God has promised that he will help any individual who asks. If a prayer appears not to have been answered, the correct response should be to ask God to help us overcome the apparent setback and show us how to grow in a positive manner. If the child in the scenario had survived the accident, but then later had died, we must realise that although God did not heal the child, he did not kill the child. It was a combination of human errors that led to the child's death, and that should be remembered. Blaming God for not intervening does not help the situation. Those affected by the situation need to pray for assistance in overcoming their grief and moving forward. Although the child can never be replaced, in most cases good can come out of a tragedy. Charities have been set up in the names of children who have died prematurely, raising vast sums of money to save the lives of other children.

Perhaps through an accident or fatal illness a husband loses his wife, who also may be the mother of young children. The prayers should be for strength to cope with the situation and support for the family. At times, this may be in the form of a second marriage, where the husband and children find happiness. I would hasten to add, that I do not believe God will have caused the death of the first wife in order that the husband can be happy with the second wife. Even if, upon reflection later, the husband feels that his second marriage is a happier one than the first, he should not believe that God caused the death of the first wife because he was preparing the way for a happier scenario. As I have mentioned previously, I believe that God does not kill anyone. Instead, God has responded to the husband's prayers by bringing good out of tragedy. As we are told in Romans 8:28, "...we know that in all things God works for the good of those who love him, who have been called according to his purpose." At times, the "good" may be better than the original situation, but that is God responding to, rather than causing, the original tragedy. It is most unhelpful when people suggest that God has initiated an evil event because he had plans to improve the situation. It is not right to believe that God would consider taking the life of anyone in order to provide greater happiness for an individual or a group of people. God is the God of love, and taking the life of any human is contrary to love.

Another fallacy concerning prayer is the idea that the greater the number of people praying for a specific outcome, the more likely it is to eventuate. It is clear that such a scenario would be most unfair. I mentioned the case of the late David Watson. He had a great number of people praying for him, and at times it was felt that the sheer weight of prayer would persuade God to cure him. David's reputation ensured that there were large numbers of people who could pray for him. There are many situations where, due to the circumstances, only one or two people are in a position to pray for a particular outcome. The success of the prayer is not dependant on the number of people praying. Nevertheless, it is also clear that if an individual has the opportunity to pray for a particular person or outcome, they should not reject this opportunity because they know that others are already praying and think one more will make no difference. God asks each of his followers to maximise their opportunities to pray. When asked, we should all pray for a particular outcome. He has invited his people to pray and so pray we must. God may well be waiting for the prayers of one specific individual before he acts.

Deepening our relationship with God through prayer

God has given us the free will to use prayer as and when we wish. As Christians, we need to remember that it is perhaps the most direct means of communication with God. By and large, Christians do not pray enough. Often the most influential Christians are those who make prayer a high priority, praying frequently and at length. We can read accounts of Christians, past and present, who have spent hours in prayer on a regular basis and developed a very special relationship with God. It is easy to find excuses not to pray regularly, but I believe that God will allow every one of his people as much time as they want, and more, to pray. If you can only spend ten minutes a day in prayer but would like to spend thirty minutes, ask God to help you find the extra time. I am convinced that he will. As with all prayers, requests need to be reasonable. If you currently spend five minutes a day praying but suddenly ask for two hours, in the hope that God may relieve you of some less desirable tasks, God may well decide that your motives need addressing before a response is forthcoming! The best way to increase the length of time spent praying is in small, manageable increments at the expense of unnecessary tasks. These tasks are usually activities that we can well do without, for example excess time in front of the television or the playing of too many computer games! If we try to achieve too much too quickly, we will probably fail miserably.

As has been demonstrated in this chapter, God can do amazing things when asked. The key is to sincerely believe that he will answer each and every prayer. Too often we pray with a vague hope that something good may be forthcoming. We lack the faith to believe that, providing our requests are reasonable and according to his guidelines, our prayers will be answered. Remember to "ask and you will receive" (John 16:4).

To conclude this chapter, I would like to share another personal experience. Like many people, I find praying difficult, and often my expectations are not what they should be.

My walking group was organising a long walk as a challenge for serious walkers on a Sunday. I had volunteered to walk out the route the day before, in order to check that there were no last minute hitches. During the week leading up to the walk, heavy rain was forecast for the weekend. I certainly did not want to do the walk in the rain. One day during the week, I had felt a strong prompting to pray that despite the weather forecast, both days would be fine enough for the walks. On the Saturday the forecast continued to predict heavy rain, although not quite as much as had originally been anticipated.

I decided to wear my waterproof clothing and take additional kit with me in case the weather should change. This necessitated the larger of my two rucksacks, which conveniently had a strap that I could fasten around my stomach. Into this strap I could tuck the plastic folder with the route directions, which was attached to a length of cord that I had around my neck.

Half an hour into the walk, it actually stopped raining, but it was still breezy. I took off the wet-weather gear and had an excellent walk. Had I taken the smaller rucksack, which I normally use, the folder with the route directions would have annoyed me, as there was no means of securing it and therefore preventing it flapping around in the breeze. God had not only answered my prayer regarding the weather, but he had also ensured that I had the correct equipment to enable me to enjoy the walk and achieve my objectives. Incidentally, the forecast for the Sunday was still not good, but it turned out to be another day with minimal rain. The whole incident was of little consequence, but I had experienced a real prompting to pray, even though it had seemed to be a waste of time, and I had been pleasantly surprised. God uses the most trivial of incidents to not only increase our faith but also to ensure that we keep the lines of communication open.

There are no specific demands from God regarding prayer. Although Paul instructs us in 1 Thessalonians 5:17 to "pray continually", God has given us the free will to decide how much time we wish to devote to prayer, how often we will pray and exactly what we will request in our prayers. He has given us guidelines as to how to pray effectively in the Lord's Prayer (Matthew 6:13-19) and it is an individual choice as to how we interpret and follow these guidelines. Rather than being rigidly prescriptive about prayer, God has given us the free will to make our own decisions.

The aim of this chapter has been to show that God responds to prayer in different ways. As God has given his people the free will to communicate with him as and when they wish, so, in return, we must accept that God has the right to respond to our prayers in the manner in which he in his wisdom knows is most appropriate. Even though our requests may not always be in the best interests of others or ourselves, God's responses always will be. We need the faith to believe this even when the immediate response may seem to dash our hopes and aspirations. As C.S. Lewis says in *The Problem of Pain*:

> *The intimacy between God and even the meanest creature is closer than any that creatures can attain with each other ... Human will becomes truly creative and truly our own when it is truly God's.*[25]

How then are we, as Christians, to ensure that our will is God's will? How are we to behave as Christians? These questions are addressed in the next chapter.

---

[25] Lewis, p.29, 90

CHAPTER SEVEN

Living the Christian Life

So, a new Christian has decided to accept the fact that God exists, Jesus Christ was crucified and rose again on the third day to redeem us from our sins and that this monumental event has opened the gate to eternal life. What now?

God shows us how he expects us to behave, but apart from the fundamental beliefs and an obligation to love one another, the precise details of exactly what we should do with our lives is often not clear. Not everyone is called to be a missionary! However, we must realise, as C.S. Lewis says in *The Problem of Pain*:

> *When we want to be something other than the thing God wants us to be, we must be wanting what, in fact, will not make us happy.*[26]

We are advised to read the Bible, communicate with God and seek counsel from fellow Christians as to what we should do in specific circumstances. Even then, we have the free will to ignore that advice. God will, however, intervene if there is a specific outcome that he desires.

The Bible states that if we believe in Jesus Christ, our sins will be forgiven and we will inherit eternal life. The first reward is eternal life, which is gained through faith in the existence of God and his Son, Jesus Christ. The next phase in the allocation of the rewards that await us in the next life relates to our achievements in this life. All Christians believe that their ultimate destination is heaven, but several passages in

---

[26] Lewis, pp.40-41

the Bible, for example, "For the Son of Man is going to come in his Father's glory with his angels, and then he will reward each person according to what they have done" (Matthew 16:27), Luke 6:35 and Ephesians 6:8, speak of God rewarding us for the good we do in this life. In 1 Corinthians 9:24-27, Paul says that we are all running a race and that we should "run in such a way as to get the prize ... a crown that will last for ever". It appears that how we live as a Christian may well affect what happens once we have inherited eternal life. Each Christian has the free will to do as much or as little as they wish to achieve these rewards.

A new outlook

There is, then, more to belief than simply believing. We are expected to change as a person and have a new outlook on life. Loving God and loving our neighbour become the focus of our lives. Exactly what this means to each Christian is very different. This is where free will plays an important role. All Christians read the same Bible and yet there are hundreds of different denominations. If the message is the same, then why is this so? Without exploring this in great detail in this book, it is sufficient to point out that having accepted Jesus Christ into our lives, we have the free will to determine exactly how our new-found faith will affect our lifestyle. We can choose a branch of the church or Christian denomination that suits us and the way in which we wish to worship God. Some prefer a more rigid and traditional approach to worship, others a more liberal and spontaneous approach.

Although all Christians have this choice regarding their response to God's calling and how much it will affect their lives, I would like to consider some ways in which those who become Christians should contemplate changes.

Changing our outlook on life also involves a possible change in lifestyle. Sometimes God may intervene directly, as we saw in the life of Paul. He may speak to an individual so powerfully that there is a complete change in direction regarding their future. For example, we only have to consider the life of the late Dr Martyn Lloyd-Jones. He trained to be a doctor but God called him to become a minister in the church and give up his medical practice. This is a significant demand when someone has spent years training to be a medical practitioner, but Dr Lloyd-Jones appeared never to question the call and was actually able to use his medical knowledge when the need arose. He felt that the call was so strong that it could not be resisted. Not everyone is called in such a way. Most Christians are required to continue in their current employment so that there are Christians in all walks of life: bankers, nurses, teachers, factory-workers, refuse collectors, etc. Christians can be very powerful witnesses in the workplace.

It is probably appropriate to introduce a note of caution here. Sometimes those recently converted to Christianity have experienced such a sense of euphoria that they wish to pass this on to their friends and work colleagues immediately. They have then been over-zealous, only succeeding in alienating those whom they wished to convert. It is important to pray carefully before embarking on any form of evangelism, to ensure that it is being done God's way. We have been given different talents, which God expects us to use in different ways. Not all are called to be evangelists. It may be our attitude to fellow workers and the way we conduct ourselves that leads to colleagues asking questions that open the way to discussing our beliefs. As Brother Andrew rightly says in his book *Light Force*, "We shouldn't expect non-Christians to read the Bible. We are the Bible non-Christians read. We are God's epistle, and everyone should read our lives."[27]

There are certain changes in lifestyle that most Christians would agree are necessary if we are to love God and love our neighbour. One of the most important is an endeavour to eliminate sin from our lives. The total elimination of sin is impossible. Circumstances are such that this was possible for one person and one person only, Jesus Christ. There are many passages in the Bible where we are asked to try to eliminate sin where possible, for example, "Therefore do not let sin reign in your mortal body so you obey its evil desires. Do not offer any part of yourself to sin as an instrument of wickedness..." (Romans 6:11-14) and, "Everyone who sins breaks the law ... No one who lives in him [God] keeps on sinning. No one who continues to sin has either seen him or known him ... The one who does what is sinful is of the devil ... anyone who does not do what is right is not God's child" (1 John 3:4-10). For those who have broken the law or who have deliberately made life difficult for someone, the way forward may seem very apparent. However, the majority of the population may well regard themselves as upright citizens who have never committed any

[27] *Light Force* by Brother Andrew and Al Janssen, p.248

heinous offence. I mentioned earlier that God considers all sin to be evil no matter how grave the nature of that sin in the eyes of the individual or society as a whole. I have also used examples of law-breaking in relation to the rules of the road and VAT that appear to have become acceptable in the eyes of many people.

We have all sinned

Jesus is actually very tough on the subject of sin, so we must first recognise that despite what non-Christians may think, we have all sinned in some way. There are certain habits and practices in all of us that need to change. Jesus made some bold statements about sin. He regards all sin as equally evil. For example, in Matthew 5:27-28 he states that lusting after a woman is as bad as committing adultery. Therefore, thoughts as well as actions need to change. This is why it is said that each individual is accountable to God and to God only. Apart from us, only God knows our thoughts and, consequently, only he can judge an individual. There is more about judgement in Chapter 9.

What is the correct reaction to what we might regard as trivial sins? Can we exceed the speed limit, as mentioned in Chapter 1, when the road is deserted and the action affects no one? As Christians, we are instructed to be positive examples. Earlier in this chapter, I included a quote from Brother Andrew suggesting that Christians are the "Bible" that non-Christians read. If we are known to have exceeded the speed limit under one set of circumstances, might not this be understood by others, Christians or non-Christians, as licence to exceed the speed limit under a different set of circumstances where the risks are greater? In the scenario we looked at in Chapter 5, where the driver of a car misjudged the situation thereby killing the child, I feel certain that this driver would never have imagined causing such a tragedy by exceeding the speed limit. Would Jesus not say that breaking the speed limit with no particular consequences is as bad as breaking the speed limit and killing a child? The actual sin is identical in both cases. It is the consequence of the sin that has changed. Often in our society, the consequences of a misdemeanour are more important than the misdemeanour itself. If a speed camera catches us breaking the speed limit we receive a fixed penalty. If the excessive speed causes a fatal accident, the punishment is far greater. It is important for Christians to think as God thinks. Although the consequences of any sin are important, it is the sin itself that is more significant in the eyes of God. God does understand that it is easy for anyone to be momentarily distracted and exceed a speed limit. It is, however, imperative that we, as Christians, do what we can to abide by the laws of the land under all circumstances.

God will forgive any sin, as long as an individual sincerely repents and turns from that sin. However, a Christian cannot deliberately break the speed limit repeatedly without there being any punitive consequences. Eventually there is likely to be a nasty surprise! Although I discuss forgiveness later, it is worth pointing out that forgiveness does not necessarily mean the avoidance of consequences. Under some circumstances, God may decide that the perpetrator has shown sufficient genuine remorse that the event will not recur. By and large, all people, including Christians, should expect some type of discipline. The Bible states that God will discipline those he loves. For example in Hebrews 12:5-11 it says, "Do not lose heart when he rebukes you, because the Lord disciplines the one he loves ... If you are not disciplined – and everyone undergoes discipline – then you are not legitimate, not true sons and daughters at all ... God disciplines us for our good." Sometimes discipline is necessary to ensure that the misdemeanour is not repeated. Sometimes it is necessary as an example to others. I discuss discipline again in Chapter 9, but it is sufficient to point out here that God says that he forgives our sins and we should put the misdemeanour behind us and move on. Although this is what God promises, unfortunately we live in a society that, for various reasons, does not always do likewise.

There are many other misdemeanours that both Christians and non-Christians tend to regard as trivial. It is worth considering another such example. There is the dilemma surrounding the concept of taxation. Some people are in a position where they are able to manipulate the amount of tax that they pay. There seems to be a general idea that "fiddling" the taxman is quite acceptable. Some may even justify the "fiddling" by giving the money saved to charity! We may think that some taxes are unfair and VAT excessive, so avoiding some tax payments may be considered acceptable. Tradesmen will often accept cash payments so that paperwork is unnecessary and the payment of VAT can be avoided. This is not what Jesus would have done. He clearly stated that everyone should pay all taxes that are due: "Give back to Caesar what is Caesar's, and to God what is God's" (Matthew

22:17-21). Christians should make every effort to pay all taxes that are owed. I will return to the issue of taxes when considering judgement.

Controlling ourselves

It is perhaps our emotions that are the biggest problem when it comes to sin. God asks us, as Christians, to think before we act in order that our actions are acceptable to him. Unfortunately, our emotions all too often get the better of us. It is so easy to become angry when something happens that annoys us. Things can happen quickly, and it is easy to react rashly before discovering the reason behind a particular occurrence. It can be most embarrassing to reprimand someone for their words or actions only to find out that the circumstances were such that the words or actions were indeed justified. If we react immediately, we will often say something that we regret at a later stage. The longer we take to react the more likely we are to act in the appropriate manner and respond rationally. I will return to this later when discussing the concept of judgement in Chapter 9.

It has been suggested that counting to ten before reacting can be of assistance under these circumstances. I would suggest a quick prayer asking God to provide the appropriate response would be preferable. There are times when it is correct to be angry. The reaction of Jesus to the money changers in the temple illustrates such a case: "When Jesus entered the temple courts, he began to drive out those who were selling. 'It is written,' he said to them, '"My house will be a house of prayer"; but you have made it "a den of robbers"'" (Luke 19:45-46). It was a deliberate response to a situation that Jesus rightly determined was unacceptable. Perhaps an appropriate example today would be the exploitation of children. The majority of people consider child exploitation to be wrong. However, before we seek to blame individuals, we need to consider carefully the facts and the circumstances surrounding the situation. It is easy to blame the parents for allowing their young children to work under any circumstances, but very often even the pittance that these children are paid is significant income for the family. Removing the children from the place of work may place families in deeper poverty. Solutions need to be found to help the families and not just the individual children. It is very easy to misread the situation and cause further problems. If anger over a specific situation is justified, the most appropriate course of action is to pray, asking for God's assistance in rectifying the situation. Anger needs to be steered in a positive direction.

Living the Christian Life

Regarding sinful actions or thoughts, God knows that we are imperfect and that we will inevitably fall short of his standards, but he does expect us to take appropriate steps to eliminate sin from our lives. The real test of what we do or think is the reaction we would expect from God if we came face to face with him after the event. If we are content with the fact that God knows our thoughts and actions and we feel that we have nothing to hide, then we are probably heading in the right direction. If you feel this is too abstract, you should consider whether you would be happy telling a fellow Christian exactly what you have done or thought. If you believe that what you have done or thought would be seen as acceptable by a fellow Christian, then it is likely that God too would find it acceptable. We have the free will to do as we like, but it is good practice to use fellow Christians to test our thoughts and actions. It is not difficult to persuade ourselves that a particular thought or course of action is justifiable or harmless, because that is what we wish to think. It may be Satan and not God who is prompting these thoughts or actions. Testing them on fellow Christians will often reveal hidden motives and a desire that does not originate from God.

Giving

Another issue that is important to all Christians concerns the help they give to others. The early Christians appear to have been incredibly generous with their time, possessions and money. They were continually helping those in need. Christians today, too, should help others. Although many would say they are satisfied with the proportion of their income and time that they give to the church and to charities, are we really as generous as those first Christians? We have the free will to assist in as many or as few situations as we wish. We can usually help in one of two ways: we can give our time or our money. The amount of time or money we give is very much a decision for the individual based upon available resources.

A man who has ten million pounds and gives away nine million may well help many more people than a man who has one hundred thousand pounds and gives away ninety thousand. The former still has one million pounds with which to finance his affairs whereas the latter only has ten thousand. Although the gift of the former appears to be more impressive, it is the gift of the latter that shows the greater sacrifice. Financial decisions are always very difficult and can often give the wrong impression. Investment of money is considered necessary – but what proportion of our money should be invested and what proportion should be given away? We are advised to "put money away" either as part of a pension or as provision for the possible costs of care in old age. Also, if we have children we will want to provide the necessary assistance to support them and, in time, their children. We can also argue that money invested now usually increases in value and so could help more people than if given away now. We are asked to be generous with our possessions. Jesus drew attention to this when observing the widow giving away the last of her money in Luke 21:1-4.

Surely, though, God does not want all Christians to give away all their possessions and money? In some cases he does! As I mentioned earlier, there are instances where people have been moved to rely exclusively on God for their income. There are churches with pastors who rely on donations from their congregations, without which they could not exist. As with all our decisions regarding the future, we need to seek God's will in prayer. If we feel God is calling us to do something specific that may be contrary to the norm, it is advisable to share our thoughts with other Christians. It would be irresponsible for Christians everywhere to suddenly decide to give up all their possessions and rely on God for financial support. Those who have actually done so have made the commitment only after feeling a specific calling from God.

Christians are called to use their money and possessions wisely. This may well involve investing money for the future but it may also involve giving up at least part of what we have. It is worth reiterating the need to pray and ask fellow Christians for help and advice. There is no doubt that many Christians have more than they need and could easily afford to give away more than they currently donate. The word "need" is the interesting one in this context. Many Christians have items that they do not actually need but there may be a very legitimate reason for not parting with them. People do not "need" televisions and radios, but these items may well help the individual to relax or provide a means of obtaining different ideas regarding key issues, which may in turn bring about positive change.

We may feel that God has given us custody of special items – family heirlooms such as clocks and pictures. We may not "need" them, in which case they could be sold, with the proceeds being given away. However, these items can never be looked upon as necessities, so if everyone felt the desire to be rid of them, apart from museums there would be nowhere for them to reside. Ultimately museums would not have the space to house all the items, so these once-precious possessions would become surplus to requirements and worthless. In order for these items to maintain their value they must be desirable. It would appear that God must regard the ownership of some valuable items as being necessary. God is aware that valuable items will be among the possessions of certain Christians who have been entrusted with their safekeeping.

Problems arise when possessions take precedence over God. We should not become overly attached to our possessions and must be aware that at any time God may ask us to dispose of them. If we are lucky enough to have the money, we have the free will to decide how we spend it. However, we do need to be careful and steward our money wisely. Because we believe that one day we will be called to account for our actions, we need to be able to justify any purchases.

Should we as Christians be spending money on luxuries like visits to cinemas, concerts, restaurants and other special places? How much should be spent on holidays or luxury items such as special clothes? If everyone decided that a night out or spending money on pleasant holidays or buying special items were unnecessary luxuries, many people would become unemployed! There would be no cinemas, restaurants, etc. Musicians would not be required for commercial purposes. Many holiday resorts throughout the world would suddenly become white elephants. The effects would reverberate through many different areas of life. Everyone needs recreational activities in order to rest and relax. Again, excess is the problem. We must balance our needs with our desires. In fact, gala concerts and other events can raise large sums of money for charitable organisations. Praying and listening to God is required, but ultimately we have all been given the free will to make our own decisions.

I have also mentioned the concept of giving time. Giving time can sometimes be more valuable than giving money. Some people will part with large sums of money as a substitute for the giving of their time. There are those who are in full-time employment and have families to look after, who may legitimately claim that they have very little spare time to give freely to others. Hence, it is often those who are retired and whose families have grown up who volunteer their time. It is, though, quite often the busiest people who find the most time to help others. And helping others is not specifically the domain of Christians. Many non-Christians are very generous with their time, but God expects Christians to find time to help others in some way. Jesus says in Matthew 25:35-40:

> For I was hungry and you gave me something to eat, I was thirsty and you gave me something to drink, I was a stranger and you invited me in, I needed clothes and you clothed me, I was ill and you looked after me, I was in prison and you came to visit me ... Truly I tell you, whatever you did for one of the least of these brothers and sisters of mine, you did for me.

As has already been mentioned, many non-Christians are introduced to Christianity because they have observed certain traits in the behaviour of close friends who are Christians and wish to find out more. Christians, therefore, must behave in a manner that can be seen by others to be special. This should not be manifested solely in the giving of money. In fact the Bible clearly states (Matthew 6:3-4) that we should be giving in secret so that no one knows what we have given. It is through our actions that we can affect the lives of others. Our behaviour should be an example to non-Christians. We do not need trumpet fanfares to announce what we are doing, but as Jesus said in the Sermon on the Mount, "Let your light shine before others, that they may see your good deeds and glorify your Father in heaven" (Matthew 5:16).

As a slightly trivial illustration of doing something positive and possibly influencing others, I have the opportunity to do something constructive when I am out walking. I often pick up some of the debris left behind by those using the local public footpaths. These items are usually cans, bottles or wrappers. Nothing too messy! They are a blot on the landscape and can cause problems to livestock if ingested. If I did this in the middle of the night or when it was pouring with rain, my actions would probably go unnoticed, but as I tend to pick up the items during the daytime, there is the chance that people will see what I am doing. Perhaps someone will then comment upon my actions. I hope that each time I will use the conversation to point out that being a Christian I feel that I need to look after the environment that God has given us. By doing small things we can change people's lives.

Testing times

Another concept that can be difficult for all Christians is the idea of being tested. I mentioned testing when considering possible reasons for the presence of evil in the world in Chapter 4.

Although Christians have the free will to determine how to respond to their beliefs, God will also set challenges for every Christian. The Bible is very clear that the only way to grow as a Christian is to accept the challenges and respond to them appropriately, which, in turn, increases our faith. "Blessed is the one who perseveres under trial because, having stood the test, that person will receive the crown of life" (James 1:12). "Now for a little while you may have had to suffer grief in all kinds of trials. These have come so that the proven genuineness of your faith ... may result in praise, glory and honour when Jesus Christ is revealed" (1 Peter 1:6-7).

Before going further, it is important to differentiate between temptation and testing. As shall be seen when looking at the Bible in the next chapter, language can play a significant part when it comes to the misunderstanding of certain terms. There are occasions when the two words appear to be used interchangeably, but they are different and Christians need to understand the difference. It is worth remembering that it is Satan who does the tempting and not God. Temptation is the enticement to do things that are contrary to God's will, but in 1 Corinthians 10:13 we are told that we will not be tempted beyond what we can endure, and that God will provide a way to withstand every temptation. It is safe to say that most, if not all, sin emanates from temptation of some sort. Satan will do all that he can to lure us away from the true path. An obvious example of temptation is lust. Many cases of adultery originate with feelings of lust. I consider sexual temptations in Chapter 10, but sadly, at times Satan succeeds in tempting Christians in this way. There are many other temptations but I think this is sufficient to illustrate the point.

Testing occurs when God allows us to go through difficult times or face challenges to strengthen our character and deepen our faith in him. James tells us in James 1:2-4:

> *Consider it pure joy, my brothers and sisters, whenever you face trials of many kinds, because you know that the testing of your faith produces perseverance. Let perseverance finish its work so that you may be mature and complete, not lacking anything.*

Sometimes these tests may seem beyond our capabilities, but the key is always to ask God to help us overcome them.

Returning to the issue of speeding, perhaps God has decided that speeding is an issue for a particular Christian. We saw in the scenarios concerning the driver and the tractor in Chapter 5 how God can intervene to change a situation. In the first of these scenarios, the driver expected to have missed the train, but in fact the train was delayed. In the second scenario, the driver was also late but the circumstances were such that the initial consequences were disastrous. The driver had to believe that God had acted in the way that he had for a specific purpose that would be revealed in time. In the third scenario, being late for the train probably saved the driver's life. As was mentioned at the time, this may well have been because God had a special plan for his life. We need to remember during these tests that "in all things God works for the good of those who love him, who have been called according to his purpose" (Romans 8:28). God is always in control, so whatever eventuates is for the best. We must be prepared for the fact that immediate pain or inconvenience will lead to a long-term solution, where the eventual outcome is of greater benefit to the individual.

I would like to share a fairly trivial situation relating to speeding and being late, which I feel God was using to test me. One day I wanted to be home from an event by a specific time for a specific reason. The journey was lengthy, taking well over four hours. When I set off it was touch and go whether I would reach my destination in time. On each occasion that I increased my speed to "make up" time, a traffic jam appeared. In fact, by the time I was waiting in the last traffic jam I had actually abandoned the idea that I could possibly reach home in time, so I reduced my speed and did not exceed the speed limit. The traffic jams disappeared, and gradually I began to realise that I could still reach home in time. Sure enough, I arrived with minutes to spare. It may seem a trivial situation but it reinforced the obligation to trust God and not take matters into my own hands.

It appears that tests are likely to become more severe when we display the faith required to pass the easier ones. Losing our job is a classic test. It is not pleasant occurrence, and as we mature in age, the prospects of finding a suitable job tend to decrease. Even at a younger age, losing our job can have a devastating effect on our family. If asked, God will always provide a solution of some description. The response may eventuate after much beseeching, but Christians are blessed in that they have someone who cares for them. God may ensure that there are lessons to be learnt along the way. Maybe it is time to accept a job with less pay because he desires that we spend more time with the family, or maybe he is asking someone to relocate because he has a church that needs that person for a specific reason. At the time, the solution may be painful, but God has a plan, and eventually matters will resolve themselves beneficially.

In the days of the early church, Christians underwent unbelievable agonies because they would not deny their faith. There is no doubt that God has permitted some of his followers, for example Stephen and the apostles Peter and Paul, to undergo what appear to be horrendous tests and yet the faith of these people never seems to have wavered. Christians today are still tortured and killed for their beliefs in some parts of the world. Consider Richard Wurmbrand in *Tortured for Christ*, Betsy and Corrie ten Boom in *The Hiding Place* and Brother Yun in *The Heavenly Man*, all of whom suffered the most appalling ordeals, but their faith remained intact. Reading about the lives of those whose faith was steadfast in the most horrific circumstances puts our relatively insignificant sufferings into perspective. Thankfully, Christians are not all tested to the same degree, but it is useful to be aware of these situations when trying to pass our comparatively minor tests. My belief is that God gives these people a very special strength to overcome the pain and sacrifice that is involved. He can then use these individuals as positive role models for the remainder of his people. If a person can undergo extreme torture and still retain their faith in God, then God must have supplied something very special to ensure this outcome. We should remember to pray for Christians in other countries for whom torture for their beliefs is still a very real possibility.

At this point, it is worth reiterating that I believe that God will never cause someone to die for their beliefs. The fact that Christians have died and do still die for their beliefs is due to the behaviour of fellow human beings. I am convinced that when Christians are about to be martyred for their beliefs God intervenes to lessen the pain and suffering of that individual. I also believe that God will not test a follower by deliberately causing the death of another human being. In my opinion, as alluded to earlier, it is wrong to suggest to any Christian that God has caused the death of someone dear to that person as a test of their faith.

Being a Christian means that we have tests from God. As we have seen, this is part of God's plan. Overcoming these tests will undoubtedly be difficult without God's assistance, so we need to ask him for his help. Although the tests are not pleasurable, James says that Christians should experience joy through the knowledge that God has perceived them as worthy of being tested: "Consider it pure joy, my brothers and sisters, whenever you face trials of many kinds" (James 1:2). As Father Du Brul explains in *Light Force*:

> *Get ready for a harder life. You are not going to know an easier road than the one that Jesus walked. But you will know no greater joy than the joy of walking with him.*[28]

This may be a difficult concept to grasp but, as mentioned previously, without challenges in life we might think that we have no need of God.

Although being a "lukewarm" Christian appears to guarantee someone a place in heaven, this is not the ethos behind Christianity. As Isobel Kuhn says:

> *The heathen around us have not much respect or interest in a smug, ordinary Christianity. 'If it costs you nothing, what proof have you that it has any value?' is their indifferent shrugging attitude. But when they see in any life the print of the nail, they are challenged.*[29]

I have mentioned the concept of our rewards in heaven being dependent upon our achievements in this life. It is our success in coping with God's tests that may well decide the level of reward allocated. I believe also that those who have suffered more for their beliefs in this life will, in all probability, receive greater rewards in the next life, which is possibly why Paul in 1 Corinthians 9:24-27 says he is continually

---

[28] Father Du Brul in Andrew and Janssen, p.242-243
[29] *By Searching* by Isobel Kuhn, p.101

striving to receive a crown that will last for ever. This does not mean that we should deliberately set ourselves difficult tests, for example giving away all our possessions, without any notion that the request to do this may have come from God. God will only help with the tests that he initiates.

So, we can see that God expects people to change when they become Christians, but each individual Christian has the free will to decide the nature and the degree of that change. God will also expect his followers to respond to challenges or tests. Life as a Christian is not easy. God has never said it would be. In fact, life may well become more difficult than it was before we became a Christian. There is, however, one major difference. Once we have become a Christian we have someone to call upon for help. God is available to help those who believe in him.

Apart from prayer, there is another way of determining God's will and that is through the reading of his Word, the Bible. This is the subject of the next chapter.

Free Will

CHAPTER EIGHT

Christians and the Bible

The Bible is the word of God. The big question is, how should we interpret what is written? At one extreme, there are those who believe that everything is to be taken literally and at the other are those who believe it is a guide, subject to cultural norms that may have changed over the years. What we do know is that the Bible contains enough information for every Christian to function as God intends.

It is important to point out that the Bible – particularly the New Testament – is in fact more reliable as a true record of events than many other historical books and documents that are taken for granted as being true. In *The Case for Christ* by Lee Strobel, comparisons between the New Testament and other documents are discussed in great detail.

Before proceeding, I would like to stress that, despite the New Testament containing probably the most important material that confirms our beliefs, the Old Testament is also of great importance. Unfortunately, there are those who would dismiss the Old Testament as being the history of the Jewish people, with little relevance for life today. I would argue that there are still lessons to be learnt from the Old Testament. Many of the problems faced by Jesus in trying to convince the people of his day, and all people since, that he was, and still is, the Messiah, mirror those experienced by God in trying to convince his people in the Old Testament of his identity.

What lessons can we learn from the Old Testament?

In the Old Testament, God performs miracles and is on hand to assist his people when they acknowledge his presence. Perhaps the most notable of the miracles was the parting of the Red Sea. For a while, those who experienced this miracle were understandably amazed and worshipped God according to his commands. As time passed, the event receded into the background of their memories and the Israelites started to complain about their circumstances. In fact, it is quite possible that, as the years passed and those who had witnessed the miracle died, the Israelites began to doubt that the event had actually taken place. A similar predicament has occurred following the resurrection of Jesus. Those who witnessed the event were on fire in their beliefs. Now, two thousand years after the event, many doubt that it ever happened.

Also, in the Old Testament, God helped his people whenever they ceased worshipping foreign gods and returned to his ways. He never promised them that life would be easy. In fact, living in tents in the desert for a long period of time was probably very harsh. However, God met the needs of his people when they turned to him for help. In the same way, Jesus has never promised that following him will be easy. In fact, he has suggested that it will be very hard at times. Yet he is always on hand to assist when we ask him.

There are many other reasons for reading the Old Testament. Some of the stories from the Old Testament are discussed in Chapter 10, to illustrate their relevance to us today. It is important to ensure, as Christians, that we read both the Old and New Testaments.

In the rest of this chapter, I intend to highlight a few observations that I have made while reading the Bible itself, consulting Bible commentaries and reflecting on the thoughts of Christian writers. Some of the points that I discuss have been used by others in an attempt to discredit the authenticity of the Bible. I attempt to provide what I feel is the correct response to these so-called "criticisms". I am no biblical scholar, so I would emphasize that these are only my observations.

The inadequacy of language

The first point I would like to make concerns the inadequacy of language. Most people struggle for words when trying to describe events to others. We may witness a truly magnificent sunset but somehow, when we try to describe the event to others, words simply cannot paint an accurate picture. Unless we have exceptional skills at expressing ourselves, the event usually sounds mundane and those listening may wonder why the event had been regarded as so spectacular in the first place. Granted, we may not have access to the linguistic skills of some of the great writers and poets, but they too often had difficulty painting pictures with words. Although there appear to be plenty of words available, often specific words do not convey meaning in precisely the way we would want.

There are perhaps at least three problems regarding language and the Bible. The first concerns the limitations of the language in which the books were first written. In many cases, biblical scholars can only speculate as to the author of certain books, and it is not possible to ascertain the literacy level of these writers. It is very interesting to see the depths to which commentators go when they expound the books in the Bible, particularly those in the New Testament. Often individual sentences and sometimes individual words are analysed to provide a meaning for the text. This is particularly true with Paul's letters. I often wonder whether Paul chose his words as carefully as commentators believe or whether he was more concerned with the general message.

The second problem relates to the change in meaning of words over time. For instance, there were many "gay" weddings at the beginning of the twentieth century, but a "gay" wedding at the beginning of the twenty-first century is something very different! One word that is used in the Bible but has a very different meaning today, particularly amongst the younger generation, is the word "awesome". God is described as being "awesome" in Deuteronomy 7:21, 10:17, and in Psalm 68:35, which means that he is awe-inspiring, to be respected, revered and possibly feared. A youngster of today will describe an event or a film as being "awesome" meaning that it is very good. God can also be described as very good, but that was not the original meaning behind the word "awesome" as used in the Bible. Because words have changed in meaning over the years, we have translations and commentaries that need to be continually updated.

The third, and perhaps most important, observation regarding language concerns the limitations of the language into which the Bible is translated – for many of us, English. For example, a word with which we have great difficulty is "love". There is more than one word in Greek (the original language of the New Testament) for the different kinds of "love", whereas in English the one word "love" has a variety of meanings. We love our spouse, our children, our dogs, our friends, fellow Christians, God and indeed ourselves, just to name a few. By no means can we say that we love them all in the same way. Love for a spouse involves feelings that lead to a sexual relationship, whereas love for our children involves a strong but different emotional feeling. Love for a friend is again different from love for our dog. Loving our fellow Christians involves yet another form of love. Consequently, when we read the word "love" in the Bible we need to be careful to ensure we understand which sort of love is intended.

It is interesting that the notes in the *NIV Study Bible* seem to suggest that there may be uncertainty over John's use of the different Greek words for "love" in John 21:16-17. Even the command to love our neighbour needs explanation, because the word "neighbour" also has different meanings. We need to examine the context in which the individual word is being used in order to discover the meaning of the word. This is one reason why lifting individual phrases or sentences from the Bible and using them out of context can be very dangerous. By extracting phrases in this manner, it is possible to use the Bible to condone almost any behaviour. At one point in Leviticus (24:10-17), it commands that blasphemers should be stoned. Such behaviour today is obviously unacceptable, but taken in the context of Leviticus it was quite acceptable at the time. In Psalm 137:9 there appears to be a suggestion that the killing of infants is acceptable under certain circumstances.

Words in the Bible seem to convey different meanings when associated with God. An obvious example is the word "day". We read in Genesis that God apparently created the world in seven days. Later in the Bible it states that to God "a day is like a thousand years" (2 Peter 3:8), so perhaps the word "day" is being used in Genesis to convey an indefinite period of time. As was shown in Chapter 2, there appears to be enough scientific evidence to support the idea that God did not create the world in seven 24-hour days. This is perhaps one reason why we should be careful when taking parts of the Bible too literally.

In fact, the whole concept of time is very different in the Bible, particularly in the early part of the Old Testament. As was mentioned in Chapter 4, we are told in the early part of the Bible that people lived to be well over a hundred – in the case of Noah 950 years! Given that life expectancy has increased over time, this seems extraordinary. Perhaps a "year" was a shorter period of time in those days. Again, there is considerable discussion in the commentary in the *NIV Study Bible* regarding Revelation 20:2. This is not only regarding the "thousand years", which some take to be a literal period of time, whereas others think it means an undetermined period of time, but also the commentary describes three different approaches to the whole topic of the "millennium".

Within the Bible words can have different meanings when used by particular writers to illustrate distinct points. An example of this is the use of the word "milk" by Peter in 1 Peter 2:2 and an alternative use of the same word by Paul in 1 Corinthians 3:2.

It is also most unfortunate that we can often grow up with the wrong perceptions of words. I have purposely used the word "Satan" to describe the evil one, but the word "devil" is often used instead. At times, it is difficult to take the meaning of the word "devil" seriously. If someone is called "a little devil", it is usually referring to a mischievous child, rather than someone inherently evil. In fact, taken with pictures of the devil dressed in red with a pitchfork and a peculiar tail, the word "devil" engenders concepts of the ridiculous, at times even bordering on the comical.

Unfortunately, as was discussed in Chapter 4, this is so far from the truth that it becomes a very serious matter. Christians know that there is an evil force in the world. Whether this is referred to as Satan or the devil matters not, but it is certainly not to be considered frivolous or amusing.

I believe the book of the Bible that probably causes the most problems amongst Christians is Revelation. John clearly had the most remarkable experience, which he was asked to record. Putting what he actually saw into words must have been extremely difficult. There appears to be a modicum of suspicion that once John had read what he had written, he may indeed have thought that he had done the best he could under the circumstances and that it was in the hands of God to provide the appropriate guidance to future readers. John's experience appears to have been almost indescribable at times.

Limitations associated with language is just one of the reasons why it is important to keep all passages of the Bible in context and to realise that the meanings of individual words need to be considered in the light of the limitations of language and also in relation to other passages in the Bible.

Distinguishing between fact and illustration

Another point to be addressed concerns exactly what, in the Bible, are facts and what could be termed as parables or stories to illustrate a point. The first books in the Bible provide an early history of the Jewish nation and much of what has been written has been corroborated by other sources. In addition, there are books of prophecies, psalms and wise sayings, but there are also books which some people consider to be factual, while others believe them to be parables. The most obvious of these, perhaps, is Job. I personally believe the book was written as a parable to send a very powerful message regarding the ability of God to create good out of evil in someone's life, providing that they retain their belief that God is good. When we are faced with a series of disasters, we need to maintain the belief that God will bring about a positive outcome if we place our trust in him. I do not wish to provide a critique of the book of Job but I do find it very difficult to believe that any Old Testament writer could have been privy to the conversation between God and Satan that is described at the beginning of the book. "The Lord said to Satan, 'Very well, then, everything he has is in your power, but on the man himself do not lay a finger'" (Job 1:12). Whether the events actually took place or not does not detract from the status of this book. It has a powerful point to make for all Christians, which applies as much today as it did when the book was originally written. Jesus told parables in the New Testament, so why should there not be parables in the Old Testament?

The Old Testament, in particular, is full of unnatural happenings which both Christians and non-Christians find hard to accept. The danger is to endeavour to try to explain how these events could have occurred naturally, for example God using natural phenomena to achieve his wishes. Perhaps the most obvious example of this, mentioned earlier in the chapter, is the parting of the waters of the Red Sea to enable the Israelites to cross safely (Exodus 14:13-28). It has been suggested that there was some sort of tsunami that caused the water to ebb and then a huge tidal wave arrived to engulf the Egyptians who were following. Yes, this is possible, but these explanations can become increasingly far-fetched as the events appear to be more miraculous. Elijah, in 1 Kings 18:16-40, despite several gallons of water being thrown over the altar, asked God to bring fire upon the sacrifice and he obliged. The area is oil-rich and who says that the "water" thrown over the altar did not contain elements that might have assisted with the ignition. This really is stretching the imagination! For those who seek such explanations, there are events where God appears to defy nature and so they become more difficult to explain. This scenario is illustrated by the story of Shadrach, Meshach and Abednego being thrown into the fiery furnace in Daniel 3:8-30. Humans are created in such a way that they will burn when they come into contact with fire. In order for these three men to have survived the furnace, God had to override his laws of nature, so finding a natural explanation becomes impossible.

Events like these invite an alternative and more logical explanation. As mentioned earlier, God has power that human beings can never comprehend. As Christians, we have to believe that he was and is capable of overriding the laws of nature and so is able to bring about events that for human beings can only be classed as miraculous. Miracles occur in the New Testament, for example the turning of the water into wine in John 2:1-11. If we endeavour to explain the supernatural events as being anything other than miraculous, the explanations can become as fantastic as the events themselves! In fact, all genuine healing has a supernatural element and perhaps the optimum course of action is not to seek "explanations" but to accept that these events occurred because God has supernatural power.

Another problem relates to the use of hyperbole. It appears that at times things are exaggerated for emphasis. There is, for example, a passage in Matthew's Gospel (5:29-30) where Jesus appears to instruct his followers to "gouge out their eyes" or "cut off their limbs" if either their eyes or their limbs cause them to sin. There is no doubt that many Christians have sinned as a result of something they have seen. The call to gouge out our eyes, if taken literally, could produce a considerable number of blind Christians! Hopefully most people do not take this literally. There is, however, a powerful message about the seriousness and consequences of sin that cannot be ignored. In Luke's Gospel (14:26), Christians are called upon to "hate" their families. Again, this appears to be the use of hyperbole to illustrate a point regarding the necessity of establishing God as the most important person in our lives.

Interpretation

Perhaps one of the most difficult challenges faced by all Christians is the interpretation of specific passages in the Bible. There are versions of the Bible that contain excellent commentaries to help the reader with these difficult passages. These commentaries not only offer an insight into the meaning of the passages, but also provide background information and cross-references. There are passages, though, where more than one explanation is offered. In the commentary in the *NIV Study Bible*, there are three possible meanings given to 1 Timothy 2:15: "But women will be saved through childbearing – if they continue in faith, love and holiness with propriety." And there are three possible explanations offered to 1 Corinthians 14:34-35: "Women should remain silent in the churches. They are not allowed to speak, but must be in submission, as the law says. If they want to enquire about something, they should ask their own husbands at home; for it is disgraceful for a woman to speak in the church."

If biblical scholars have studied the original text and are divided as to what it actually means, then how can an ordinary layman decide which explanation represents the original message of the writer? There are also passages in the Old Testament where a scribe over the years may have miscopied something, because events do not tally, see for example the *NIV Study Bible's* commentary on 2 Chronicles 16:1 or on 2 Chronicles 31:16. If the Bible truly is God's Word, then how can there be doubts over the meaning of certain passages, and why are there small errors in transcription? In *Discipleship*, David Watson makes the point that "a good translation is not a transliteration". He offers as an example, the New English Bible's translation of 1 Corinthians 14:13: "the man who falls into an ecstatic utterance", where the literal translation from the Greek is "the one who speaks in a tongue". He states, "To describe speaking in tongues as falling into ecstatic utterance is both a wild and somewhat alarming guess as to the precise nature of the experience."[30]

I believe the answers to these biblical predicaments are in fact comparatively straightforward. The Bible has been written for every Christian. As Christians, we read the Bible in conjunction with prayer to God for enlightenment. Specific groups of Christians have different agendas. All Christians have the free will to read and interpret the Bible as they wish. If we wish to nit-pick and highlight possible inconsistencies then so be it, but that will not assist in the growth of particular individuals as Christians.

All Christians are expected to read the Bible, but not every Christian is required to be a biblical scholar. There is no doubt that God, if asked, will lead each Christian to the passages that he wants that individual to

---

[30] *Discipleship* by David Watson, p.155

read and act upon. It may be pertinent to suggest that there are certain passages of Scripture that are perhaps more relevant to some Christians than to others. Perhaps someone reading this book is about to face a series of difficult challenges or maybe even a disaster. God knows what is about to happen and may well lead that person to read Job. Perhaps a Christian has a problem with pride, then God may well focus that person's attention on passages relating to humility, for example James 4:6 or 1 Peter 5:5-6. Paul, in his letters (for example Ephesians 4:11 and 1 Corinthians 12:4-11), says that God appoints each Christian to a different role according to their gifting. He says that some Christians are called to be teachers, others evangelists, others prophets, etc. If we are called to be teachers, we need to focus on passages that illustrate the attributes of a good teacher. If we are called to work amongst the poor, we need to read passages that will strengthen us in dealing with the obstacles that may well be encountered along the way. As Christians, we need to discover our vocation through prayer and God will direct us to passages in the Bible that will help in the execution of that vocation. At times it may also be expedient to seek the advice of other Christians as to which passages may be the most relevant.

In 1 Corinthians 13:12 Paul states, "For now we see only a reflection in a mirror; then we shall see face to face. Now I know in part; then I shall know fully." God does not intend that we will understand every verse of the Bible. Some of these mysteries will only be revealed when we finally reach heaven. However, if we feel drawn to certain parts of the Bible, but are having trouble understanding these passages, we can ask God for guidance, and there are many commentaries by reputable Christian scholars that will help us. It is important to make use of these commentaries. They are an excellent aid to interpreting the Bible. These scholars have consulted manuscripts and a wide variety of sources to which many Christians do not have access, in order to explain difficult passages. I remember being puzzled by the passage in the New Testament, John 9:1-3, concerning the healing of a man who appeared to have been born blind, just so that Jesus could heal him. To me this idea seemed wrong. As intimated previously, I do not believe that God produces people with deformities solely so that he can demonstrate his powers of healing. I discovered by consulting Bible commentaries on the passage that my interpretation was in fact incorrect. The man had been born with the deformity, not because God had ordained it. Jesus, however, was able to use the situation to demonstrate his powers and bring about a positive outcome to the situation. This was an enlightened but ultimately an obvious explanation. It is often the case that when faced with these explanations, we may wonder why we had never thought of them previously! It is God's way of encouraging us to read both the Bible and Christian literature to increase our understanding of his word.

John Stott, in his book *The Contemporary Christian*, and David Watson, in his book *Discipleship*, both advise all Christians to read the Bible at two levels. When reading any passage, we should endeavour to consider which aspects have their roots in the culture of the day and which ideas relate to us today. This does not give us license to reject every idea that may be perceived to be difficult on the grounds that it may be regarded as being cultural, therefore adhering only to those that suit us individually. Of course, we do have the free will to do precisely that if we wish! I believe both writers are pointing out that there are aspects of the Bible, particularly in the Old Testament, that are culturally orientated and so not as relevant today as when they were originally written.

To summarise, I believe that the Bible is God's Word and that it is of the utmost importance to every Christian. God requires us to accept what is written, without necessarily understanding all the whys and wherefores. Each Christian has the free will to interpret the Bible in whatever way they wish, but should ask God for illumination and revelation in order to live the life that he has ordained for them. If something is important to the individual, God will ensure that there is the necessary understanding. Years and years of studying every available commentary and every translation of the Bible will not provide any one person with a definitive answer as to the precise meaning of every passage in the Bible. We are obliged to ask for God's enlightenment regarding his Word. He will ensure that those passages which we need to understand will be understood and those which we do not need to understand will remain a mystery.

CHAPTER NINE

Fairness, Forgiveness and Judgement

When we become a Christian, we often need to reassess our understanding of certain concepts. In this chapter, I will be considering the notions of fairness, forgiveness and judgement, all of which are linked in many ways.

Fairness

One concept that needs to be redefined is that of fairness. God's definition of fairness can appear to differ greatly from our understanding of its meaning. At times, this may cause a degree of conflict. Let us consider a variation of the well-known parable of the labourers in the vineyard (see Matthew 20:1-16) that Jesus told his followers.

A businessman employs an unemployed person to work for him for a day for an agreed wage. Later in the day, the same businessman employs another unemployed person to work for him for the remainder of the day, agreeing to pay him the same wage as had been agreed for the first person. At the end of the day, the businessman finds a person who has been trying to find work all day but has been unsuccessful. The businessman has pity on him and decides to give him a donation equal to the amount that he has agreed to pay each of the two workers. All three men have received identical sums of money but obviously have worked for different lengths of time. Many people would have little problem with the donation, as society accepts that donations are given to those in need. As in the original parable, it is the fact that two workers have worked for differing amounts of time but have received the same remuneration that causes the problem and leads to a feeling of injustice.

Jesus actually uses the parable to illustrate a point regarding the kingdom of heaven but there is an issue regarding the concept of fairness. The worker who laboured all day received what he had agreed to be a fair wage. The fact that the businessman chose to be generous with the other two people is surely the prerogative of the businessman. The businessman has seen a need and responded according to that need. God behaves in the same way. When considering the plight of sinners, God will offer forgiveness at any time. His people have the free will to decide whether or not to repent of their sins and follow him. The nature of the sins, the number of sins or the length of time over which they have been committed matter not in the eyes of God. What does matter is that sinners repent as soon as they realise that repentance is necessary. It is ill-advised to continue sinning and put off repentance until a later date!

There appears to be no preferential treatment for someone who has been a Christian for a considerable period of time over someone who genuinely seeks forgiveness moments before death. An individual does not earn forgiveness via the accumulation of good deeds. "For it is by grace you have been saved, through faith – and this is not from yourselves, it is the gift of God – not by works, so that no one can boast" (Ephesians 2:8-9). Because God treats his people in this way, it is never too late to repent of your sins and ask for forgiveness.

Forgiveness

The concept of fairness also arises when it comes to Christians and forgiveness. God forgives his followers each time they err and ask for forgiveness. Psalm 103:10-12 says:

> *He does not treat us as our sins deserve or repay us according to our iniquities. For as high as the heavens are above the earth, so great is his love for those who fear him; as far as the east is from the west, so far has he removed our transgressions from us.*

Not only are the sins forgiven, they are also forgotten. "For I will forgive their wickedness and will remember their sins no more" (Hebrews 8:12). Christians are asked to do likewise and forgive, not just once but time and time again. When Jesus was asked how many times we should forgive someone, he replied, "I tell you, not seven times, but seventy-seven times" (Matthew 18:21-22).

Discipline and consequences

Before proceeding further, it is necessary to reiterate that God does not suggest that misdemeanours should not be disciplined. It is worth pausing to consider some of the dilemmas concerning the whole concept of discipline. As mentioned earlier, although God forgives sins, the Bible clearly states in Hebrews 12:6-11 that those committing misdemeanours should be disciplined:

> It says ... "the Lord disciplines the one he loves, and he chastens everyone he accepts as his son." Endure hardship as discipline; God is treating you as his children. For what children are not disciplined by their father? If you are not disciplined – and everyone undergoes discipline – then you are not legitimate, not true sons and daughters at all. Moreover, we have all had human fathers who disciplined us and we respected them for it. How much more should we submit to the Father of spirits and live! They disciplined us for a little while as they thought best; but God disciplines us for our good, in order that we may share in his holiness. No discipline seems pleasant at the time, but painful. Later on, however, it produces a harvest of righteousness and peace for those who have been trained by it.

At times, the distinction between discipline and retaliation can become blurred. This can lead to problems as to when and if a Christian should intervene when a misdemeanour has occurred. Regarding such intervention, I believe there are three possibilities. Some situations should be left to God regarding any form of discipline or retribution, in some circumstances the Christian needs to provide the discipline or rebuke, and on other occasions, when laws have been broken, it is the legal system that has to become involved. Because things are never straightforward, I think it is useful to introduce some more scenarios.

In scenario A, Mr D is in a supermarket car park waiting for a particular parking space to be vacated. As soon as the occupant leaves,

109

another driver who has seen Mr D waiting pulls in front of him and drives into the vacant space.

In scenario B, Ms E has a neighbour who delights in making life very difficult for her because he knows she is a Christian and wishes to see how far he can go before she retaliates.

In scenario C, Mr F is an only child. His father has died and his mother is in her late eighties, living on her own. No matter what Mr F does for his mother, she always finds fault with him. Despite being a caring person, Mr F can do nothing right in her eyes.

In scenario D, Mrs G sees her 4-year-old son suddenly hit his 2-year-old sister for no apparent reason.

In scenario E, Mrs H sees her 4-year-old son run out into the road, having been warned several times previously not to do so.

In scenario F, Mr J on leaving a party notices his friend who has had too much to drink about to get into his car ready to drive home. Mr J tells his friend that he should not be driving but his friend insists that it is quite safe and sets off anyway.

In scenario G, Mr K is an electrician who runs his own business. He is VAT registered. There is another electrician in the neighbourhood who is also VAT registered, but is happy to do certain jobs for "cash" so that the VAT is not charged. By doing so, he can do the jobs for less money than Mr K who always charges VAT.

In each of the first three scenarios, the situation should be left to God to handle. In scenario A, it is very tempting for Mr D to get out of the car and abuse the driver who has taken the parking space for which he was waiting patiently. As with many examples of what we often call "road rage", the incident is very frustrating but little or nothing can be gained by intervention. Confronting the perpetrator often leads to a torrent of abuse, which then only serves to inflame the situation. Although it is not easy, incidents like this have to be left to God.

In scenario B, the neighbour is waiting for Ms E to retaliate at some stage. Often this situation may in fact be one of those tests from God that were discussed in Chapter 7. Unless the neighbour's actions threaten her safety or that of any member of her family, in which case the police should become involved, asking for God's help is the best course of action.

In scenario C, the temptation is for Mr F to stop helping his mother. I have noticed in my dealings with old people that they can become very frustrated and short-tempered as they grow older. Often there appears to be no obvious reason other than the fact that they are ageing. Mr F's mother will probably die without changing her attitude towards him, but he can only ask God to give him the strength to persevere. Again, this scenario could be another test from God.

In each case, despite the temptations, it would be wrong for the offended party to take action themselves. The reaction instead should be to hand the situation to God in prayer. "Do not repay anyone evil for evil. Be careful to do what is right in the eyes of everyone ... for it is written: 'It is mine to avenge; I will repay,' says the Lord" (Romans 12:17-19).

This may initially not help the situation, but we have to trust that in the long term things will work out for the best and that God will ensure that there is a feeling of peace for the aggrieved person and that the aggressor may at some stage become aware of the inappropriateness of the behaviour.

In scenarios D and E, the child needs to know that the behaviour is not acceptable. In these cases, it is not right to rely on God to chastise the child. These types of misdemeanour usually occur within the family situation or where a child is being cared for by someone authorised to do so. In scenario D, the child needs to know that such behaviour is just not permissible. In scenario E, the child needs to appreciate the possible consequences of his behaviour. Discipline needs to be administered in a loving and caring way, and for this God may need to be consulted. The Bible advocates disciplining of children by their parents (see for example, Proverbs 13:24; 19:18; 23:13-14). It is interesting that two of these references appear to advocate the use of physical punishment in a way that is now illegal in this country. Suggesting that such action is recommended in the Bible does not constitute a viable defence if used in a court of law! Taking the Bible literally in this instance is not a good idea.

In scenarios F and G, the situation is extremely difficult, but these misdemeanours contravene the law of the land and are punishable as crimes. In scenario F, the consequences of driving after having consumed too much alcohol could be disastrous, not just for the driver but also for other innocent people. If, however, Christians become vigilantes and report every minor infringement of the law to the authorities, it will not help society's perception of Christians. However, we cannot ignore the situation. Mr J has a duty to convince his friend that he should not drive. If necessary, he should enlist the help of other friends at the party. Hopefully, he would receive the support that he needs without having to take more drastic action. This situation still occurs all too frequently and provides a real dilemma for those in Mr J's position, whether or not they are Christians.

In scenario G, the position is also very difficult. Mr K can warn his competitor that he is aware of what is happening, but actually notifying the authorities may have undesirable consequences amongst potential customers in the community. Mr K can explain to customers why he refuses to waive the VAT and stress the illegality of non-payment of VAT. Unfortunately, as mentioned earlier, evasion of VAT is considered by many members of society to be perfectly acceptable. It may be very hard for Mr K to put across his point, but asking for God's help is almost certainly more effective than approaching the authorities.

Prayer is the common denominator in each of the above scenarios, but there are times when Christians have to do more than pray and we need to be aware of that. Intervening without praying can inflame the situation in any of the scenarios above. It is important not to overreact and do something that we will later regret. By praying, at least we have time to think.

How should we forgive?

Returning to the concept of forgiveness, all Christians need to remember that whatever the misdemeanour, we are asked to forgive, not once, but each time that it happens. This is extremely difficult. At times it is also contrary to what is expected in society at large. Once someone has a criminal record, in some cases it remains there for life. The offence is to be remembered. I do not propose to discuss the pros and cons of the criminal justice system in depth, but there is no doubt this does create a dilemma. Obviously some criminals have no intention of changing their ways. From these people society needs to be protected. There are some offenders who are genuinely repentant and would like the opportunity for a fresh start, but with a criminal record this can be very difficult. Should the church be more proactive in helping these people, despite the possible risks? Faced with the realisation that a criminal record remains with the perpetrator of the crime for life, some offenders may decide it is easier to lead a life of crime rather than try to "go straight", which makes a mockery of the rehabilitation schemes.

If an offender becomes a Christian and genuinely repents of his crimes, how are other Christians supposed to react? The obvious answer is that they are to forgive and offer support in assisting the person to move forward and start a new life. Unfortunately that is not always straightforward. If an offender has a drinking and driving offence or has been imprisoned for some financial irregularity, a new start may well be possible. What is to be the reaction of the Christian community to a sex offender? For many reasons the community cannot simply forgive and move on as if nothing has happened. Crimes like these offer special challenges to Christians who, on the one hand, are urged to give the new Christian every opportunity to lead a "normal" life but who also, on the other hand, need to be aware of the potential consequences of having such a person in their community.

It is easy to recommend prayer as an aid to forgiving, but what about those whose loved ones have been killed by terrorists, drunk drivers or any other individual? Can they genuinely forgive the perpetrators? The answer is "yes" but only with deep faith and much help from God. There have been several high-profile examples of forgiveness. The father of the girl killed in Enniskillen by an IRA bomb forgave her killers. He also became very involved in the peace process in Northern Ireland. The father of the young boy killed by another bomb in Warrington also used the situation to seek a resolution to the conflict. There have been many other examples, and there is no doubt that genuine forgiveness under these circumstances has a dynamic effect on those whose lives are touched by it. With God's help, Christians can tap into this power.

Often the circumstances of the killing make forgiveness extremely difficult. In the scenario discussed earlier, where the young boy was knocked over and killed, there is more likely to be forgiveness because it was a genuine accident and the perpetrator would have shown genuine remorse. If the killing is deliberate, as in a gangland feud where the perpetrator intended to kill the victim and there is no remorse, then forgiveness is exceedingly difficult. If there is genuine repentance and change in the perpetrator, forgiveness is more likely.

The Holocaust was mentioned earlier. Corrie ten Boom, who tells her story of her time in a concentration camp in *The Hiding Place*, found it exceedingly difficult to forgive one of the perpetrators, even though he wished to be forgiven and became a Christian. It was actually Corrie's sister, Betsie, who had the deeper faith and managed to see

God's hand in the most appalling situations. We only have to read about the lice in the concentration camp and other horrors they faced to realise the strength of Betsie's faith.

It has been suggested that we, as Christians, should love the sinner but hate the sin. This can be extremely difficult, and yet there are examples in life where this happens regularly. How many times does a loving mother forgive her children for their misdemeanours, some of which may be very serious?

When considering forgiveness at any level, we need to return to the cross. Christ knew that those crucifying him were well aware of what they were doing. They were inflicting extreme suffering on an innocent man. They were not sorry for what they had done, and yet Jesus in all his agony forgave them. If we genuinely love someone, forgiveness is less difficult. This is why God asks Christians to love not only one another but also non-Christians. By endeavouring to love the individual and hate the sin, we can hopefully begin to forgive. The more serious the nature of the misdemeanour, the longer it will take to forgive, but with God's help through prayer, anything is possible. We have the free will to react as we wish, but in the long term, if we can forgive, we will feel stronger and more at peace. Clinging to a refusal to forgive harms the one who has been wronged far more than it does the perpetrator of the original sin.

It is worth remembering the words of Brother Andrew, "Forgiveness is the key that opens your enemy's heart." He also has strong words concerning our "enemies":

> As long as we see any person – Muslim, Communist, terrorist – as an enemy, then the love of God cannot flow through us to reach him. Each of us has a choice. I can go to terrorists and love them into the Kingdom. And the moment I love them they are no longer my enemy.

He goes on to make a decisive statement when asked, who is the enemy? He responds, "The devil! Never people!"[31]

The fact is that all Christians have God to help them forgive. We have an advantage over other members of society. God has never said it will be easy, but he is there to help when asked.

---

[31] Andrew and Janssen, pp.248, 229

Judgement

Related to the issue of forgiveness is the idea of judgement. This is another concept with which Christians appear to have problems. God has clearly stated in the Bible that he alone is to judge, see for example the letter of James 4:12: "There is only one Lawgiver and Judge, the one who is able to save and destroy. But you – who are you to judge your neighbour?" And Jesus says in Luke 6:37-38: "Do not judge, and you will not be judged. Do not condemn, and you will not be condemned. Forgive, and you will be forgiven."

Christians are told not to judge. It is, though, extremely difficult not to judge others. This can vary from criticising the actions of an individual over a fairly minor misdemeanour to condemning what appears to be a major atrocity. Jesus tells us in Matthew 7:3-5 that we should remove the plank in our own eye before considering the speck in someone else's eye.

It is worth considering another scenario at this stage. A group of Christians are visiting one of the developing world countries. They are walking in the street, when suddenly a young teenage boy rushes round the corner and collides with them. He is obviously very frightened, and when they question him, they realise that he has stolen food from the local market. So, being honest people they apprehend him and march him along the road to the nearest police station. On the way, they meet the local priest who asks them where they are going. They tell him about the boy and how they are seeing that justice is done. The priest then says to them, "If there is any one of you who has never exceeded the speed limit when driving your car, or who has never failed to pay VAT by offering cash in hand, then let them take this boy to the police station."

One by one, the Christians walk away and leave the priest with the teenager. "Young man," he says, "I know you are hungry but what you have done is wrong. Mend your ways, trust in God and in future never take something that is not yours."

Of course, this is very similar to Jesus and the adulteress in John 8:1-11. It does highlight a very important issue. As Christians, we are very quick to condemn a variety of events, including those that appear to be obviously unacceptable, like the Holocaust. Although we can rightly be outraged by such events, we must not judge the perpetrators. That is the prerogative of God and God alone.

Where judgement is so divisive is when it occurs within the Christian church. This can be seen with the issue of homosexuality. I do not intend to discuss the theological arguments, but would like to make a few points. Like all other Christians, a Christian with homosexual inclinations can read the Bible and will discover the passages that appear to condemn homosexuality. He then has the free will to pray to God and interpret the passages as he sees fit. If he feels that the passages do not relate to homosexual relationships in this day and age then so be it. He has the free will to ignore them, and other Christians should accept his decision even though they may disagree with his assessment of the situation. They can express their feelings, but they cannot condemn his actions. As mentioned in the previous chapter, the interpretation of biblical truths is between the individual Christian and God. If any Christian has chosen to ignore any aspect of Scripture, the decision they make is between them and God. Every Christian will be held accountable for the decisions they make.

Unfortunately, the Christian church has been beset by schisms over the years. Certain Christians judge others to be wrong and so form a new denomination of the church. Although efforts are being made to reconcile some denominations, unity within the church has been almost totally destroyed, and non-Christians find it difficult to understand why those belonging to a religion that preaches love and tolerance appear not to be able to worship together. All Christian denominations believe, I hope, that Jesus Christ is the Son of God, was crucified and then rose again from the dead, and that as a result, those who believe in Jesus and genuinely repent of their sins have eternal life. The Christian faith is built upon these foundations.

Denominations have been created due to disagreements over secondary issues. Unfortunately, this has usually happened because Christians have disagreed on issues such as the way that they conduct their worship, transubstantiation or infant baptism. Of course, when we examine in detail the history of the Christian church we can see that it is riddled with actions that have been taken in the name of Christianity but have actually been carried out for other, often political, reasons. New denominations have at times been established as a result of opposition to such actions. There were many reasons for the new denominations that were inaugurated during the Reformation period, but the one uniting factor was a belief that the Catholic Church had strayed from the true Christian path. It is right that at these times fellow

Christians express their doubts regarding the established church, but is it necessarily correct to split the church by forming a new denomination?

It is interesting to note that the Church of England, as we know it, actually has its origins in the desire of Henry VIII to divorce his wife, Catherine of Aragon. Obviously, there were other issues which contributed to a very complex situation, but fundamentally, that is why the sovereign is head of the Church of England. Had Henry VIII not wanted to divorce his wife, things may have been very different. Some Christians would still argue that no person, sovereign or otherwise, has the right to be head of any church.

I am a great fan of the late Dr Martyn Lloyd-Jones, but I do not agree with his frequent criticism of various beliefs associated with the Roman Catholic Church. I believe that he should have declared that he disagreed with certain issues but should then have affirmed that the judgement of such issues is the prerogative of God alone.

It is interesting that some of those who founded new denominations never intended these churches to break away from the established church. Both John and Charles Wesley, for example, never wished Methodism to be established as a rival denomination to the Church of England. I believe we, as Christians, can worship in any Christian church, even when we do not necessarily agree with every idea of that particular denomination (provided that it does not violate the basic fundamentals mentioned above), because worship is between the individual and God. I believe that it is of greater importance to emphasise the issues that unite rather than divide the church. It is an irritating fact of life that the media delights in highlighting the divisive rather than the uniting issues in the church.

There is another very good reason why judgement should be left to God alone. We often misinterpret the situation and make fools of ourselves. He never does! There are times when we can become angry regarding a specific situation without knowing all the circumstances surrounding that situation. Another scenario illustrates this point.

Miss P has been in a queue that has formed on the inside lane of a dual carriageway for traffic that is actually going straight ahead at the next roundabout. The outside lane is for traffic turning right. She has been in the queue for some time and is at last nearing the roundabout. As the traffic moves slightly, Miss P reacts rather slowly. This provides the ideal opportunity for a car that has jumped the queue to pull in front of her. Naturally, she is furious that a queue-jumper has behaved in such a way, avoiding the need to wait in the queue. This happens frequently at junctions and can be most irritating. Although each queue-jumper only delays those in the queue by a few seconds, the combined effect of a significant number of interlopers can produce a considerable delay. We might assume that Miss P has a right to be annoyed, but consider the actual plight of this particular queue-jumper.

The driver is actually travelling in this area for the first time. He has planned his route using a map. He knows that he has to follow the road for some distance before turning off. He then notices traffic in the inside lane slowing down and so he moves to the outside lane, suspecting that the traffic in the inside lane will probably be turning left. It is only after he has passed a considerable section of the queue that he spots a signpost indicating that he must be in the left-hand lane if he wishes to go straight ahead at the next roundabout. It is at this point that he has to find a gap in the queue. This he finds in front of Miss P. He tries to wave a thank-you, but realises he has probably between mistaken for a queue-jumper.

I have experienced a similar misunderstanding of a situation myself. I have sold items on behalf of a community overseas. There has always been a notice explaining that all money taken at the stall is paid directly to the women who make the items, but on occasions, customers have failed to read the notice and wrongly insinuated that I have been exploiting the women for my own personal gain.

Often we do not have a clear picture of the circumstances surrounding a particular event. What appears wrong may not in fact be so. It is important to ascertain all the facts regarding a given situation before making any assumptions. God is never wrong, so leave it to him to judge.

Regarding the three concepts discussed in this chapter – fairness, forgiveness and judgement – it is often difficult for Christians to act in the way that God intended. His requirements are very clear but may challenge our natural desires. We have the free will to react in whatever way we wish, but we must realise that God has specific reasons for asking us to respond in a certain way. He is always right and knows that responding in the manner that he commands will ultimately ensure that we grow in a positive way as Christians.

CHAPTER TEN

Sexual Activity and War

I have decided to include this short chapter on sexual activity and war, because these are two areas where I believe that society has strayed from the teachings of God and Jesus in such a way that the consequences have been disastrous.

There is little doubt that the greatest source of temptation in human beings relates to sexual activity. I will be devoting the first part of the chapter to this subject, showing that sexual freedom is not as condonable as society appears to advocate.

Throughout history, one of the most mistaken beliefs has been that nations can settle their differences through conflict and violence. In the second part of the chapter, I will be considering the limitations of war when attempting to resolve disputes between nations.

Sexual activity and God's standards

It is difficult to dispute the fact that, in our world today, we have considerable sexual freedom, provided that two conditions are observed: both participants consent to the sexual activity and the sexual act is not carried out with a minor. I have touched upon same-sex liaisons in the previous chapter and these are not addressed in particular in this chapter.

The Bible appears to advocate that we should indulge in a sexual relationship with one person and one person only. This relationship should be entered into in order to express our love for our partner by consummating a marriage. There are many passages in the Bible that contain instructions regarding marriage, for example 1 Corinthians 7.

Marriage is regarded as the sole means of committing ourselves to a life with a partner that is binding until the death of one member of that partnership. In today's society, couples are reluctant to make the necessary commitment and consequently prefer to live together without legalising the union.

There are passages in the Bible that denounce adultery and divorce, for example, Matthew 5:27-32. In society today both adultery and divorce have become widely acceptable. Those who are married are free to divorce when they tire of each other or when one or both members of the partnership decide they wish to cohabit with someone else. Our "promiscuous" society permits all sexual relationships provided that they are consensual and neither party is a minor.

Pressure to consent

It is perhaps the concept of "consent" that creates a multitude of problems: for example, can a young girl who has drunk too much alcohol be in a state of mind such that she can consent to a sexual encounter? There is also no doubt that teenage girls are and have been for some time under enormous pressure to consent to sexual relationships, often against their better judgement, with consequences that can be disastrous.

I was teaching at a girls' school in the 1980s. I remember an attractive girl of 15 or 16 expressing her anguish that the boys with which she was associating were without exception looking for one thing – a sexual encounter. She desperately wanted to meet a boy with whom she could enjoy a close but non-sexual relationship. Tragically, she failed to find such a boy, and within a few months committed suicide.

Unscrupulous boys can persuade girls, by using a variety of tactics, that a sexual encounter will enhance a relationship. The boys may express "undying love", or simply persuade the girls that refusing a sexual encounter is paramount to saying that the supposed passion felt by the boy is not reciprocated. Eventually, against her better judgement, the girl may submit to the boy's requests with tragic consequences. The girl may then be "dumped" by the boy who moves on to seek another "conquest". She may feel "dirty" or "used". Emotionally she may be distraught. With the advent of the internet, social media is such that details or even pictures of the sexual encounter can be broadcast within minutes. Such revelations may further embarrass, or in fact be used to blackmail, the girl. There is no doubt that the girl has used her free will to consent to the activity, so no action can be taken to prevent the boy from repeating his behaviour.

It is interesting that perhaps the first recorded example of total rejection on the part of the male perpetrator after a sexual encounter occurs in the Old Testament. It is a story that can be found in 2 Samuel 13. It is not particularly well known. In the story, Amnon has a burning desire to have sexual intercourse with his half-sister, Tamar. He engineers a situation where he finds himself alone with her. He then rapes her. Immediately afterwards we find this verse: "Then Amnon hated her with intense hatred. In fact he hated her more than he loved her." This is a sobering illustration of the way in which some men treat women.

It is of course true to say that the situation is sometimes reversed. There are many examples throughout history where important men have been undone by the advances of unscrupulous women, one very notable example of which occurred during the 1960s when a minister in the government was forced to resign after an illicit affair.

There are at least two occasions, again in the Old Testament, where men have been betrayed by deceitful women. In Genesis 39, Joseph refused to be drawn into a sexual relationship with the wife of Potiphar, one of the Egyptian officials. The woman was so frustrated at having been rebuffed that she engineered a situation where she accused Joseph of attempting to rape her – an offence for which Joseph was unjustly imprisoned.

In Judges 16, Samson became besotted by Delilah. The Philistines, who were desperate to know the source of Samson's great strength so that they could subdue him, bribed Delilah by offering her a large sum of money if she could persuade Samson to reveal his secret. It is actually a very tragic story because, initially, Samson resisted Delilah's requests by imparting false information. He had the opportunity to see through her seduction, but ultimately he yielded to her wishes because he was completely infatuated.

There is no doubt that sexual temptation is very strong. There are, of course, examples of sexual encounters to which both participants have obviously fully consented. We may wonder why these are wrong.

Sexual relationships outside marriage

If one or both parties in the encounter are already in a supposedly stable relationship with another person either married or unmarried, news of this liaison will inevitably reach their partner or partners. The result will be distressing for the injured party but could have more far-reaching consequences if there are children involved. The effects that such affairs have on the immediate family are often totally disregarded.

How often has a marriage been devastated by the liaison between a married man and a female member of staff in his office? There is no doubt that working in an environment where two people who share a mutual attraction see each other every day provides huge temptation. No member of staff can initiate the dismissal of a fellow worker simply because they are tempted to have an illicit sexual relationship! Unfortunately, the desire is strengthened if the object of that desire appears to respond to any advances, whether genuinely or manipulatively. The affair should be resisted, otherwise others will be hurt. The solution is to bring the matter to God and pray for assistance in overcoming the urges and temptations.

In Chapter 1, I spoke of selfishness as being the motive for many actions. There is no doubt that this is very true in the case of sexual encounters. As mentioned before, a family can be devastated by the selfish actions of one of its members who has decided to put their sexual desires before the feelings of the family. Unfortunately, today's society condones such behaviour. Again, there is an excellent example of the consequences of an illicit affair between two consenting parties to be found in the Bible. It is the story of David and Bathsheba in chapters 11 and 12 of 2 Samuel. David has sexual intercourse with Bathsheba who, despite being married, appears to be a willing partner. Unfortunately for David, she falls pregnant. David tries unsuccessfully to persuade Bathsheba's husband to return from the battlefield and sleep with her in an attempt to cover up what they have done. However, he declines to do so and so David has her husband killed in a fabricated situation during a battle. David is shown the error of his ways by the prophet Nathan, who uses a delightful parable. David and Bathsheba marry. Although David repents, he has to live with the consequences of his actions. Their son dies soon after birth and David has to witness infighting amongst his offspring, one of whom was Amnon, already mentioned in the story about Tamar.

Lust versus loving commitment

There is no passage in the Bible that specifically states that sex before marriage is forbidden, although in 1 Corinthians 7:1-2 Paul seems to be alluding to this when he says:

It is good for a man not to have sexual relations with a woman. But since sexual immorality is occurring, each man should have sexual relations with his own wife, and each woman with her own husband ... If they cannot control themselves, they should marry, for it is better to marry than to burn with passion.

Sexual relationships are not supposed to result from feelings of lust. They are intended to be the product of a loving commitment. The Bible views lust as sinful (see 1 Thessalonians 4:3-5 and Colossians 3:5). Another point to stress is that if a sexual relationship is purely lustful, there is always the possibility of the "Tamar effect". Following the first sexual liaison, what has up to that point been an excellent non-sexual relationship between two people can be destroyed by sexual activity that is in some ways disappointing or unfulfilling.

Unfortunately, lust is a powerful motivator for sexual relationships, but such relationships seldom endure unless accompanied by love. We live in a society that condones the type of sexual activity which is contrary to what is advocated in the Bible. If all sexual activity was confined to married couples in loving relationships, many of the problems initiated by what is termed "casual sex" or "one-night stands", the majority of which are a result of lust as opposed to love, would disappear. Although we have the free will to do as we wish, God's way is best.

War

The second part of this chapter is devoted to the concept of war or any form of violent confrontation between nations. Throughout history, nations have decided that the most effective way to exert their power over others is to do battle with them. The tactic has been used to acquire more land by overrunning other nations. It has also been used to settle disputes within nations. Empires have been created by various superpowers, which have subdued territories and established control over vast areas of land. Obviously, countries do not appreciate being subdued, so ultimately these empires are challenged. They wither and are replaced by others. Eventually, nations oppressed by others regain their freedom. Territories are annexed temporarily. This was particularly true in the Second World War, but is also true of one of the last great empires, the British Empire, which has gradually disintegrated as its territories have been granted the right to self-rule.

War in the Bible

There is a major problem regarding war and the Bible. The Old Testament appears to condone war, as was discussed in Chapter 8. God seems to encourage his people to attack, defeat and often annihilate various tribes so that his people can live in the "promised land".

It can be argued that the indigenous peoples that were defeated were engaging in abhorrent and obscene practices. They were so entrenched in their ways and so reluctant to put an end to these practices that God had no choice but to overrun them and in some cases actually annihilate them. Whether this was actually why God initially decided to choose this territory for the Israelites we do not know. We also have to remember that culturally circumstances were very different at that time. God may have decided that war was the only option. We must accept that God had his reasons for doing what he did.

The way of Jesus

In the New Testament, with the arrival of Jesus, things changed. Jesus had a very different message. War and conflict were to end and be replaced by peace and love. The Jews knew that the Messiah would come, but they expected him to be a warrior similar to someone like Joshua. The Messiah was expected to lead the Jews in a revolt against the hated Roman occupation. They would then become masters, once again, of their land. Yes, of course Jesus could have done this. His achievements may have lasted as long as the Roman Empire. He could have been another Julius Caesar. However, empires do not last – so what would have happened once he had died and some other superpower had swept into prominence?

Jesus' way was different. It is interesting to pause for a moment and consider how long his movement has lasted. It has been around for more than two thousand years and shows no signs of disappearing. No other empire or movement has survived for that length of time. What does this tell us? It points to the fact that, yet again, God has a plan that is far superior to anything proposed by humankind.

Granted, Jesus' way is not as dramatic as war. It may well take longer to win over people through peace and love, but the effects are deeper and longer lasting. We only have to read Richard Wurmbrand's story in *Tortured for Christ* to understand the power of love. Despite the most horrendous circumstances, some of which were unprintable, he managed to show peace and love to his persecutors – to the extent that many became believers.

When acts of war or terror are perpetrated, there is still a burning desire for revenge and retribution. As Christians, we need to show that despite feelings of anger and bitterness, there is another, better way.

When Jesus arrived in this world, his main aim was to demonstrate how people could live in peace and harmony, even when living under a foreign power. He too showed that he had power, but it was to be used in a different manner. He performed miracles and healed the sick. He used his power to draw attention to his way of life. There was the danger that the people might expect him to perform even greater miracles and lead them in an uprising against the Romans. Jesus did not want the Jews to recognise him as the Messiah before his death and resurrection. As a result, he went to considerable lengths to ensure that he did not reveal his true nature to anyone other than those for whom there was a special reason. On occasions, he warned his disciples not to disclose his true identity to the people: "'But what about you?' he asked. 'Who do you say I am?' Peter answered, 'God's Messiah.' Jesus strictly warned them not to tell this to anyone" (Luke 9:20-21).

It is also interesting to highlight the fact that there were no political speeches. Jesus was happy to criticise the Jewish leaders, but he never spoke out against the Romans. He also made no comments regarding issues which today we may see as unacceptable, for example slavery. He focused entirely on his mission. When the Pharisees attempted to trick him, he managed to produce a response that could not be perceived as controversial, for example Matthew 22:15-21:

Then the Pharisees went out and laid plans to trap him in his words. They sent their disciples to him along with the Herodians. "Teacher," they said, "we know that you are a man of integrity and that you teach the way of God in accordance with the truth. You aren't swayed by others,

125

because you pay no attention to who they are. Tell us then, what is your opinion? Is it right to pay the poll-tax to Caesar or not?"

But Jesus, knowing their evil intent, said, "You hypocrites, why are you trying to trap me? Show me the coin used for paying the tax." They brought him a denarius, and he asked them, "Whose image is this? And whose inscription?"

"Caesar's," they replied.

Then he said to them, "So give back to Caesar what is Caesar's, and to God what is God's."

He was cautious and yet determined. He pursued a policy that nations and factions within the nations would be wise to adopt today.

Two thousand years later, the world remains adamant in its belief that it knows better and refuses to heed his advice. Unfortunately, we live in a world where the various factions in society imagine that the most effective way to highlight their demands or promote their cause is through violence. As has been discussed, this may work over a short period of time, but will ultimately fail. As Christians, we need to promote the approach that Jesus initiated. Every now and again there is the smallest of hints that Jesus' way can find reconciliation when all else has failed.

By and large, any form of reconciliation between Palestinians and Jews has failed. It is little more than a pipe dream. Brother Andrew, as recorded in his book *Light Force*, made a concerted effort to bring together Palestinian and Jewish Christians. The initial meetings were traumatic because of the inherent problems between the nations. Once they began to share their common beliefs, lasting friendships were established. God has demonstrated that there is a solution, but realistically there is little chance of its success given the strong cultural traditions that are so much a part of the conflict. It would require the conversion of the majority of both the Jews and the Palestinians to Christianity.

In this chapter I have attempted to highlight two aspects of life that create problems, both needing prayer and change. Individuals need God's assistance in overcoming sexual temptations that lead to sexual liaisons contrary to what is recommended in the Bible. Nations and the various factions within those nations need to realise that every individual has a right to life and that conflict involving killing is not the way forward. In the long term, it will never succeed. The way forward is that advocated by Jesus – the way of peace and love.

Free Will

Conclusion

Just as you have the free will to reject everything that I have written in this book, God has given you the free will to involve him in as much or as little of your life as you wish. His ultimate aim is that all Christians should give their lives to him so that he can use them in the way that he desires. He has, however, given each individual the free will to decide exactly how much of their life they will surrender to God.

The first step is for the individual to decide whether they believe that God exists. Revelation 3:20 says, "Here I am! I stand at the door and knock. If anyone hears my voice and opens the door, I will come in and eat with that person, and they with me." It is a decision that every individual has to make and there is no direct pressure from God – although, as we have seen, there are times when he does intervene.

If we decide that God does exist, then there are implications regarding the effect of this decision on the remainder of our lives. We have to change, but we are free to decide the degree to which we will change. God says that if we believe, our sins will be forgiven and we will inherit eternal life. For some, this may be sufficient and they may decide to do little else. However, there is no doubt that God expects more than this and there is the whole concept of his judgement. In Chapter 7, I pointed out that "everyone will have to give account on the day of judgement" (Matthew 12:36) and justify the decisions we have made during our lives. I also discussed the possibility of the existence of a system of rewards relating to the way we have conducted our lives while on earth. Although the exact nature of these rewards may be unclear, it does appear that we should expect to receive some degree of recognition that acknowledges the actions we have taken or the sacrifices we have made.

There is no doubt, then, that Christians are expected to do more than just believe, although eternal life depends on belief alone. Being a Christian is supposed to have an impact on our lives. We are expected to grow as a Christian, and there are specific ways in which this can be done.

In order to develop as a Christian there are four specific things that will assist us in our growth in the Christian faith.

First, we should pray. As discussed previously, there are excellent books written to guide the individual in this process. Prayer is our primary means of communication with God. Christians must pray so that God will reveal what he has planned for each individual. Being receptive to God's will is not easy. It takes practice and patience. The Bible contains many passages asking us to pray and, of course, there are references to Jesus praying on a number of different occasions. If Jesus prayed, and the apostles prayed, then we too must also pray.

Second, we should read the Bible. The Bible is God's Word. It is probably profitable to ensure that at some stage we take time to read the whole Bible. There are some passages that are difficult to understand, and sections that appear to have little meaning in today's world, but it is beneficial to have an overall picture of the contents of the whole Bible. Christians can rest assured that God will not ask them to dwell on passages that are obscure or have no relevance to their Christian lives. I believe it is actually an advantage to follow a Bible study course on a daily basis. These courses often follow themes and generally have excellent commentaries to help interpret God's Word. However, these daily readings should not be our only encounter with the Bible. Additional sections need to be read on a regular basis so that we become familiar with the book.

Third, Christians need to be part of a Christian community. There are those who say that they have their own relationship with God and do not need to belong to a local church. However, Christians need support from one another if they are to grow in their Christian faith. They need to communicate and worship together on a regular basis. God asks us to worship him. Although it is possible for us to worship on our own, it is easier and usually more effective as part of a larger group. Being a member of a church often means we can attend regular Bible-study groups. This ensures additional encounters with God's Word; it gives us the opportunity to discuss the more complex issues, and often results in the resolution of issues that have become problematic.

People usually join their local church because they wish to be part of the local Christian community, but it is important to feel drawn to the church where we worship. We need to be comfortable with the congregation, the type of service and the leader. If we ask him, God will lead us to the church that is the most appropriate for us. It is not a good idea to change churches too often. It is important to discuss with our church leaders anything with which we disagree, and to resolve any problems whenever possible. It is preferable to air our views within that church so that changes can be made if it is felt to be appropriate. Continually changing church may indicate a problem within the individual Christian that needs to be resolved, rather than an issue with any particular church. It is, however, quite healthy to visit other types of church once in a while to experience different types of worship. There is something awe-inspiring about attending sung evensong in a cathedral with its own choir and choral music. There is something particularly joyous about attending an evangelical service which has its own singing group, but where the congregation may participate more fully.

Fourth, it is useful to read Christian literature in addition to reading the Bible. I have found it very informative to read books about the lives of influential Christians whose experiences are inspirational. I have also found it enlightening to read books by well-known Christian writers. These may be commentaries on the books of the Bible or they may be expositions on Christian issues such as discipline, heaven or prayer. Our own church community can be limited in its ideas, thoughts and explanations, so it is useful to be acquainted with the ideas of Christian writers who have been moved to put their thoughts and beliefs into print. Christians past and present have insights into the many different aspects of Christianity, and there is a wealth of information to be discovered by the reader. However, we must learn to consider carefully what we read; no Christian writer is infallible, and we should always ensure that what we read is compatible with what is written in the Bible.

This book has been about free will. God could have decided that humans should not have free will, but I believe if he had, life would have been mundane and predictable. By giving us free will, God has issued a challenge. He has provided us with sufficient resources to live our lives as he would want. We have the means and assistance to do so, but he does need to be involved. He has, through free will, ensured that each individual has the power to accept or reject his challenge. We must remember that his desire is that everyone will believe in him and follow his way.

It is a poor thing to come to him as a last resort ... If God were proud he would hardly have us on such terms: but he is

> not proud, he stoops to conquer, he will have us even though
> we have shown that we prefer everything else to him, and
> come to him because there is "nothing better" now to be
> had.[32]

The Problem of Pain, C.S. Lewis

It is worth concluding by reiterating that Jesus stated that he is the only way to eternal life, so if you choose to reject him you need to be very certain that you are making the right decision. If you reject him and you are wrong, the consequences may well be dire. It is perhaps appropriate to finish with Pascal's Wager.

In *The Case for God*, Peter Williams discusses what has been called Pascal's Wager, a summary of which follows.

We have two choices: to believe in God or not to believe in God. There are two possibilities regarding God – either he exists or he does not. There are therefore four possible outcomes:

- We believe in God and he exists.
- We believe in God but he does not exist.
- We do not believe in God and he does not exist.
- We do not believe in God and he does exist.

If the first outcome is correct, we receive a prize of inestimable value. If the second outcome is correct, death is final but we have probably not missed out greatly by believing mistakenly that God exists. If the third outcome is correct, death is final but nothing has been gained or lost. If the fourth outcome is correct, the outcome could be catastrophic.

God has given you free will, so use it wisely!

---

[32] Lewis, p.85

Bibliography

Alexander, Denis, *Creation or Evolution* (Oxford: Monarch, 2008).

Andrew, Brother, *God's Smuggler* (London: Hodder & Stoughton, 2008).

Andrew, Brother & Al Janssen, *Light Force* (London: Hodder & Stoughton, 2004).

Deibler Rose, Darlene, *Evidence Not Seen* (Milton Keynes: Authentic Media, 2011).

Grubb, N.P., *C.T. Studd, Cricketer and Pioneer* (Cambridge: Lutterworth Press, 2014).

Kendall, R.T., *The Thorn in the Flesh* (London: Hodder & Stoughton, 1999).

Kendall, R.T., *Pure Joy* (London: Hodder & Stoughton, 2004).

Kendall, R.T., *God Meant it for Good* (Milton Keynes: Authentic Media, 2011).

Kirkby, John, *Nevertheless* (Bradford: Christians Against Poverty, 2008).

Kuhn, Isobel, *By Searching* (Milton Keynes: Authentic Media, 2011).

Langmead, Clive, *Robber of the Cruel Streets – The Prayerful Life of George Muller* (Farnham: CWR, 2006).

Lewis, C.S., *The Problem of Pain* (New York: Macmillan, 1944).

Lewis, C.S., *Mere Christianity* (London: Geoffrey Bles, 1952).

Lloyd-Jones, Martyn, *Studies in the Sermon on the Mount* (Nottingham: IVP, 2002).

McGrath, Alister E., *Christian Theology – An Introduction, 5th edition* (London: Wiley-Blackwell, 2011).

Morison, Frank, *Who Moved the Stone?* (Milton Keynes: Authentic Media, 2012).

Murray, Iain H., *The Life of Martyn Lloyd-Jones (1899-1981)* (London: Banner of Truth Trust, 2013).

Pawson, David, *Unlocking the Bible* (London: Collins, 2007).

Stott, John, *The Contemporary Christian* (Nottingham: IVP, 1999).

Strobel, Lee, *The Case for Christ* (Grand Rapids, MI: Zondervan, 1998).

Strobel, Lee, *The Case for Faith* (Grand Rapids, MI: Zondervan, 2000).

Ten Boom, Corrie, *The Hiding Place* (London: Hodder & Stoughton, 2004).

Watson, David, *Fear No Evil* (London: Hodder & Stoughton, 1984).

Watson, David, *Discipleship* (London: Hodder & Stoughton, 1999).

Williams, Peter S., *The Case for God* (Oxford: Monarch, 1999).

Wurmbrand, Richard, *Tortured for Christ* (Orpington: Release International, 2011).

Yun, Brother & Paul Hathaway, *The Heavenly Man* (Oxford: Monarch, 2002).

Similar Books from the Publisher

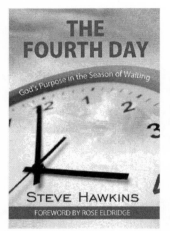

The Fourth Day
Steve Hawkins
ISBN 978-1-910197-53-0

Only God can fathom the countless intricacies of how He works in our lives, whether we happen to see ourselves as currently prospering or finding life somewhat a trial.

We think we know how God should act – but how do we respond when the outcome is not what we expected? We do our best: we think, we reason, we may pummel our brains or seek advice. But there is a better way for us...

Beginning with the account of the death of Lazarus and Jesus' delay in visiting him until the Fourth Day, Steve unpacks why God allows us to face seasons in which He may seem absent and not act in the way we expect. He demonstrates how we can pass through these difficult times with God's reassuring peace and eternal perspective.

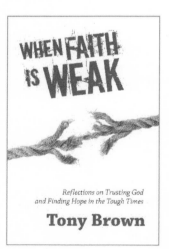

When Faith is Weak
Tony Brown
ISBN 978-1-907509-91-9

Why is life so difficult at times? Why does God not seem to be there when you need him most? Why don't things work out the way we expect?

In the ebbs and flow of life, when faith is tested and times are tough, we need to rediscover our confidence in God who patiently understands our fragility, freely forgives our sins, graciously restores our strength and lovingly lifts us to new heights of service.

Each chapter of this book is concerned with a particular problem or issue that every Christian will probably confront at some point in their life. The overriding message is that however we feel and whatever experience we face, God will never reject or abandon us but in his perfect time will bring to completion what he has begun.

Available now from your local bookshop or *onwardsandupwards.org*